date
er
v

The Island Imagined by the Sea

About the Author

Kieran McNally is an Irish writer and historian who has written on the history of medicine in journals such as *History of Psychology*, *History of the Human Sciences*, and *History and Psychiatry*. He lives in Clontarf, Dublin.

THE ISLAND IMAGINED BY THE SEA

A History of Bull Island

Kieran McNally

Illustrations by Jean Shouldice

The Liffey Press

Published by
The Liffey Press Ltd
Raheny Shopping Centre, Second Floor
Raheny, Dublin 5, Ireland
www.theliffeypress.com

© 2014 Kieran McNally

A catalogue record of this book is
available from the British Library.

ISBN 978-1-908308-58-0

Printed in Spain by GraphyCems

Contents

1. A Severed Arm   1

2. A Long Finger   4

3. Shipwrecked   10

4. Captain Bligh   17

5. A Known Art   21

6. The Island the Sea Swallowed   24

7. Vikings: The Raven's Banner   29

8. The Botanists   35

9. Dead Leg Beats Sprained Ankle   38

10. The Wooden Bridge   40

11. Crab Lake, Oysters   45

12. A Pestilent Swamp   53

13. A Consummate Bibliophile   57

14. The Nightingale and the Mermaid   62

15. The Meadow of the Bull   66

16. Lady Kane   69

17. The Sand Witches   73

18. Kid Gloves   77

19. The War on Birds   81

20. The Crow's Nest   92

21. Bathing Waters   97

22. Curley's Hole   101

23. Found Drowned   106

24. The Actor   109

25. 'You Have Insulted Us'   110

26. Sanctuary   115

27. A&E   121

28. The Fog   122

29. Fishing in the Underworld   126

30. Lost and Found   131

31. The Bird Girl   137

32. The Blue Lagoon   141

33. The Causeway   148

34. Mice, Fleas, Foxes, Hares   152

35. Fire and the Alder Marsh   158

36. View from the Beach   170

37. Flotsam and Jetsam   172

38. Bad Chemistry   177

39. Art Deco   181

40. Star of the Sea   184

41. Bottle Quay   187

42. The Seals   190

43. Biosphere   193

44. An Old Salt   197

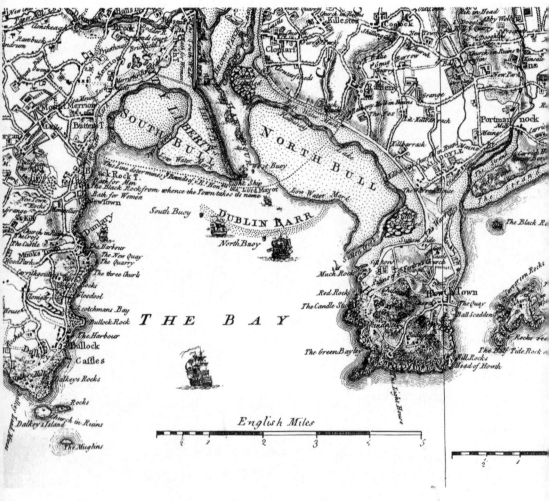

A Map of Dublin Bay by John Rocque, 1762

A Severed Arm

This island was made for poets. When the vagrant wind sweeps through the quaking grass it ruffles the mythical blue hare and the European rabbit. It jostles the marsh and honeybee orchids. And on the foreshore, its breath lifts the sands into scattered wisps that swirl and dance through the dunes and cord grass. All over the island, lovers drift and stray.

The air is sonorous with the shuffle of waves and cries of migrant birds. It is heavy with the scent of the sea and its salt marshes. On bad days, at the southern end, nutrients in the water give rise to brown algae that comes ashore and putrefies. On good days – if you know where to look – there are the more subtle scents of buckthorn, sea lavender and lilac trees. But there are not many trees on the island. Certainly scattered through the grasses and elsewhere are a few such as sycamore. And at the northern end of the island there is the Alder marsh, so-called because of a smattering of Alders dispersed through the area. But that's about all.

Somewhere near the Alder marsh with its black bog rush and lady's smock someone once found a severed arm. The Gardaí made a public appeal for information. Nothing useful came of it. Interpol later identified the arm using DNA. It belonged to a convicted rapist, James Nolan. In the month prior to the arm's discovery, Nolan had been released from Dublin's Mountjoy Prison. After his release, Nolan was never seen again. It was rumoured that his associates hated him enough not to bother reporting him missing. On bad days the island seems wind torn, rain swept and desolate. It is a lonely place to find an arm.

Public speculation on the fate of Nolan took two lines. The first suggested that Nolan's enemies, who were numerous, had him killed and dumped in the bay. The second was that Nolan was full of remorse and self-loathing. He jumped from one of the Liffey's bridges on a night of swollen currents and drowned. His body was then swept out into Dublin Bay. In both stories, the propellers of a passing ship chopped his body up. The gouged arm was washed up on the beach and taken into the marsh in the jaws of a dog. For all the speculation the body has never been found. Officially, Gardaí are still looking for a man with one arm.

But then not everything is easy to find. Hidden over the mudflats, the dunes and the marshes are many species of plants. Some rarities include the red hemp nettle, the petalwort and the meadow saxifrage. Others like the alders tongue are very small. The smallest is an eyelash in length. And its secret location is known only to botanists. Other plants have names like Yorkshire fog, crested dog's tail and devil's bit. They are not hard to find, but since people do not know how to recognise them, they remain unarticulated and mostly invisible. The honeybee orchid is surely the most interesting of these. It has evolved to look as if a bee sits on its pink petals, but the bee does not exist.

A Severed Arm – Notes

In 1977, a green algae was also present and thought to have been characteristic of polluted water. Other species characteristic of unpolluted water were also present. The sand is blacker on the southern end as a result of decaying organic matter (Jeffrey, 1977).

The Alders were described as stunted in 1955 (Odlum, W.P., 'Bird notes from the Bull Island', *The Irish Naturalists' Journal*, 11(11), 309); about 200 existed in 1977. The marsh is also home of the snail killing fly (*Pherbellia cinerella*) and the gloriously named cuckoo spit bug, whose frothy blobs can be seen on grass stems as detailed in the Bull's most important scientific monograph (Jeffrey, D.W., Ed., 1977, *North Bull Island – Dublin Bay – a modern costal natural history*, Dublin, Royal Dublin Society).

On lady's smock (Goodwillie, R., Ni Laimhe, E. and Webb, R., 1988, *A Second Report on Areas of Scientific Interest in County Dublin*, Dublin, Dublin City Council).

Reports concerning sexual crimes on the island are not unknown. In 1979, one Paul Reilly was charged with attempted rape of one woman and indecent assault of another (Anon., 1979, December 11, *Irish Press*, p. 5). Child prostitution on the northern end of the island is also known to have occurred quite recently.

2

A Long Finger

The story of the creation of what the *Freeman's Journal* described as 'a long finger of an island' is fairly well known. Dubliners had long sought to alleviate silting at the mouth of the river Liffey. But dredging alone had been ineffective. So the Ballast Board built two long walls – north and south of the Liffey – to keep its channel from choking. After a number of false starts, and almost a century of work, this human intervention more or less succeeded, with one pleasant consequence: sand backed up against the North Bull Wall. After that the sand continued to accumulate, and over two centuries it formed an island – Bull Island. In 1871, the island was estimated at just over 1.5 miles. Today it measures more than twice that. It emerged off the north Dublin Bay coast, just off Clontarf, an area more famously associated with a bloodbath inflicted on 'Vikings' in 1014 by the Irish high king Brian Bóru, who seemingly lost his head in the process.

For Dubliners then the island has existed for little over two centuries. But such a claim – like fishermen's tales – must be taken with a pinch of salt. For prior to the North Bull Wall's construction, an outline of this nascent landmass *already* existed. In 1686, for example, one Captain Greenville Collins marks the North Bull as 'a hard Sand dry at low water'. Much as it does today, this dry sand already arched along the coast as far as its natural limit: Sutton Creek at the foot of Howth, the peninsula north of Dublin Bay.

In the next century, more references to this mass of sand can be found without difficulty. In 1786, for example, William Wilson's gloriously titled *Post Chaise Companion* marks the North Bull as 'a most dangerous lee shore'. This wind-ravaged shore extended to Sutton from opposite the house of one Eustace near Clontarf. It is not known if any of this sand was visible at high tide in the 1780s – historians are often stumped for the want of a platitude – but by 1800 it is indisputable: there definitely seems to have been a small but permanent dry patch. And by 1819 an area known as Sand Island was mapped as a long strip of island (at least 3 kilometres long). Its cartographer, Francis Giles, later refers to it as 'The Green' or 'Bull Island'.

As such the North Bull sands were already a significant fixture in the bay's topography – prior to the North Bull Wall's construction. Indeed, part of the rationale for the North Wall's build, at the 'west end of the Sand Island', was to *prevent* the Bull Sands from clogging the harbour. Rather than being *created* by the wall, this island's westward growth was actually impeded by its construction. In folk memory, truth is sometimes a mere technicality.

Even less well remembered is the fact that there was once more than one island. Beside the main island, a group of several smaller islands, known as the Bull calves, are also known to have existed. These eventually merged into each other. The last to 'disappear' at the Sutton end of the island was known as

Green Island. It seems to have first appeared around 1862 and was gone by 1902. As the name suggests, it was covered thickly with vegetation; for a time aficionados could still identify it by the continued presence of the Bull Island's only creeping willow – friend of the white satin moth and willow warbler.

A Long Finger – Notes

On a long finger (Anon, 1921, June 29, *Freeman's Journal*, p. 3).

The Ballast Board was incorporated in 1707 under the title The Corporation for Preserving and Improving the Port of Dublin. About 1714, the Liffey was embanked on both sides. Quays were built and marshy ground 'reclaimed'.

The North Wall was built between 1819 and 1824. The South from 1753-1780, although from at least 1715 oak piles imported from Wales were used (Corry, G., 1970, 'The Dublin bar: The obstacle to the improvement of the port of Dublin', *Dublin Historical Record*, 23(4), pp. 137-152).

The North Bull Wall also lead to a sandbar known as 'the mumbles' being created near the mouth of the Liffey, and partial bars during construction, but these were removed by dredging (Anon., 1836, *Parliamentary Papers, House of Commons and Command*, Vol. 24, London, H.M. Stationery Office). The 'North Spit' sand bank – present in 1818 – was gone by 1833.

Dollymount forms the coastal area adjacent to the island and was once used for swimming. For this reason the island's beach is also known as Dollymount strand.

On island length (Godkin, J. and Walker, J., 1871, *The New Handbook of Ireland*, Dublin, Dublin Steam Printing Company).

The island in now roughly 5 kilometres long by 1 kilometre wide. Worn stones on the Bull Wall record the wall length in feet.

On the 1686 map by Collins, the water south of the North Bull sands is known as the 'Iron Poole'. The earlier Down survey mapping of 1658 appears to show both sand (dotted but unlabelled) and no sand, possibly reflecting tides. Elsewhere Hendrick Doncker's 1658 *Paskaarte om achter Yrlant om te zeylen, van Hitlant tot aen Heÿssant* clearly shows the North Bull sands. Later, Frederik de Wit's 1700 *Regni et insulæ Hiberniæ delineatio in qua sont Lagenia, Ultonia, Connachia et Momonia provenciæ* also appears to show dotted sand (Library of Congress). Pieter Van Den Keere's 1605 *Map of Leinster* shows Howth as a separate island. The isthmus had not yet formed (British Library).

Clontarf stretches for a number of miles on the coast out of Dublin. The areas nearest Bull Island, known as the Sheds or 'Herring Sheds', was once a fishing village. In 1534, the residents of Clontarf enjoyed the rights to fish in far off Carlingford tax-free. During the 1641 crisis, Sir Charles Coote, following the spirit of his written orders, burnt the houses of one George King (who had tried to levy every barrel of herring landed at Clontarf Strand in 1620). This occurred at Clontarf on the fifteenth of December with 16 deaths, supposedly because locals were rebels who had plundered an English 'bark', but it may also have been partially motivated by the fact that it was an economic rival to the port at Dublin (boats were to be captured or sunk) and just general revenge for King's involvement in the 1641 events at Swords (Curry, J., 1793, *An Historical and Critical Review of the Civil Wars in Ireland,* Dublin, P. Wogan). Clontarf had a monastery in 550 AD, supposedly founded by St. Congal.

On the dangerous lee shore (Wilson, W., 1786, *The Post Chaise Companion*, Dublin, J. Fleming).

Bligh's map shows the dry patch. A map by 'Cowan' may also have shown it. The dry bank on Cowan's map was described as less than half a mile long (Anon., 1924, January 29, *Freeman's Journal*, p. 8). McIntyre notes that Richard Broughton confirmed its existence above high tide in 1801 (McIntyre, Dennis, 1987, *The Meadow of the Bull*, Dublin, Future Print).

Tidal currents seem to have ensured Sand Island was an island and not simply an accumulation of sand backed up against the coast.

In 1819, Giles would propose a railway crossing Sutton Creek and building a railway along the northern shore of the island, to ferry stones from Sutton in the building of the wall (De Courcy, J.W., 1996, *The Liffey in Dublin*, Dublin, Gill & Macmillan).

On preventing clogging (Anon., 1836, *Parliamentary Papers, House of Commons and Command*, Vol. 24, London, H.M. Stationery Office).

Some believe that the emergence of the North Bull sands may have been due to the building of the South Bull Wall. Certainly this wall's construction and interference with tides, though laboriously planned, was in many senses experimental – its precise consequences on tides and sands were not predictable. So the South wall *may* have caused the emergence of Sand Island some years later. But strictly speaking this can't be verified. Either way, as we shall see, the sands probably pre-existed both walls and were not a product of the North Bull Wall (Flood, D.T., 1975, *Dublin Historical Record*, Vol. 28, No. 4, pp. 142-153).

Gillmore's chart of Dublin Bay shows three possible islands or 'calves' at the tip of Bull Island in 1881 (Moore, N., 2008, *Dublin Docklands Reinvented*, Dublin, Four Courts Press).

In 1917, creeping willow (*Salix repens*) is thought to have originated from seed borne winds from Portmarnock

(Anon., 1917, 'Irish societies', *The Irish Naturalist*, 26(10), pp. 166-168).

The white satin moth was actually only recorded for the first time in 1992, on grey willow (*Salix cinerea*) and the Alder marsh. It is not thought to have been present earlier (Wistow, S., 1992, 'The white satin moth (Leucoma salicis(L.)) Lepidoptera, New to Co. Dublin', *The Irish Naturalists' Journal*, 24 (4), 167).

3

Shipwrecked

South of the island, ferries now pass peacefully to the Isle of Man, Holyhead and Liverpool. It was not always this way. Dublin Bay has been notoriously insecure for ships over the centuries. Between 1796 and 1803 *alone* over 124 vessels were damaged in the bay – with numerous lives lost. When combined with the howling breath of the Gods, the Bull's lurking sands posed a significant component of this environmental challenge to seafarers. In 1799, for example, *The Penguin* was wrecked on the Bull. Sixty-five bodies washed ashore. In August 1803, *The Paragon* of New York and *The Beresford* similarly struck on the North Bull in a severe storm. The celebrated Cornish tenor Charles Incledon was among those found and saved in 'the shrouds'. Even secured vessels weren't safe. In 1798, a tempest drove two ships from their anchor and ran them on the North Bull. A crew of 14 – fleeing in a boat – were lost in the surf.

Understandably then, for centuries prayer was a readily used technology. In fact, the Abbey of Kilbarrack, en route to Howth and overlooking the island, was supposedly built 'on the strand near the great sand bank called the North Bull, for the assistance of shipwrecked mariners'. And for this reason, mariners paid a fee to it right up to around 1538 – before the reformation halted it. It is not clear when this practice commenced. The church originates from the twelfth or thirteenth centuries but a much earlier church of St Berac also existed.

Of course, prayer appeases neither nature nor man. In 1524, Archbishop Allan's boat was stranded on the sands at Clontarf after fleeing Dublin's Damesgate at night. His pilot was accused of a lack of skill and perfidy – because he had links with Allan's enemies – even though a deliberate beaching would surely have been a dangerous undertaking. The emotive accusation is nonetheless understandable: Allan had been captured naked in hiding and hacked to death by his killers. And perhaps echoing these events, a 1790 map from Clontarf's Vernon Estate indicates a small channel on the Bull sands at low tide named 'Allen's channel' (along with ten wrecks).

A sand bar to the south, on which the South Wall was eventually constructed by 1760, also presented a significant obstacle to boats, as did a sand bar that blocked entrance to the Liffey. Collectively, these sand bars were sufficiently obstructive to force boats to anchor out in the bay at low tide. They then waited for a high tide to carry them across – as was the case with diarist's Anne Plumptre's boat in 1814. All this reminds us of an uncomfortable fact. The frailty of human technology in the North Bull area stretched much more than half a millennium in recorded history alone – in spite of undeniable progress in the science of shipbuilding and navigation.

Humans and their ships were not the only things to get stranded on Dublin's sands. Particularly unlucky were the school of porpoises and bottlenose dolphins that stranded on the North Bull in 1716. All forty-two had their flesh partially

hacked by 'country people' (it smelt like fat pork). Equally unfortunate was the 'monster of the deep' encountered by fishermen in 1846. Stranded in low water, the 14-foot long creature
was a 'brilliant sea green'. It had five fins. Its tail was forked
like a salmon. Its teeth were described as sharp as needles. The
monster – a shark – was captured with oars. It was brought
into town and exhibited. Sharks were and remain rare in Dublin waters (so when one Mrs Doran found the skeleton of a
boy in the sea by the Bull Island Coast Guard Station, with
both arms and right leg detached, he was as likely to have been
nibbled by ordinary sea creatures as any monster of the deep).

As the nineteenth century progressed such vivid, visceral
and celebratory contact with nature was passing for Dubliners. With its opening in 1831, the Zoological Gardens in the
Phoenix Park would begin a process that would successfully
corral Dubliners into more formalised encounters with nature. Hence, already by 1839 seals (alive on the island today)
had been sent to the Portobello Zoological Gardens. And so by
1931, when a pilot whale was stranded on the Bull, it was boxed
and sent to the Natural History Museum without much ado – a
small group of his bones can still be found in a glass display
cabinet on the island's visitor centre. Science had seemingly
detached itself from over excitement. Yet for all that, through-
out the twentieth century the island became increasingly used
by Trinity College and other educational institutions as an
outdoor university. A living island remained a tangible and
incomparable mentor. And the odd squid, starfish, seahorse,
triggerfish and jellyfish, which continued to be found stranded
on the shore, remained a necessary emotional stimulant.

Shipwrecked – Notes

On disasters between 1796 and 1803 (Wartburton, J., Whitelaw, J. and Walsh, R., 1818, *History of the City of Dublin*, London, Cadell and Davies).

Danger to ships also came from scrimping on pilotage costs (Anon., 1873, January 4, *Freeman's Journal*, p. 2).

Charles Incledon in the shrouds (i.e. the sails) (Anon., 1803, *The Scots Magazine*, Edinburgh, Alex Chapman).

Boats were not always accidentally lost. In 1749, three 'gabbards' struck the Bull after being set loose maliciously from Georges Quay (Anon., 1749, March 13, *Belfast Newsletter*, p. 3).

On the crew of 14 (Anon., 1798, *The Gentleman's Magazine*, Vol. 68(2), 1076).

On the great sand bank (Norie, J.W., 1839, *The New British Channel Pilot, Containing Sailing Directions from London to Liverpool*, London, Navigation Warehouse).

On church of St Berac (Lewis, Samuel, 1837, *A Topographical Dictionary of Ireland, Volume 1.*, London, S. Lewis & Co). The current churchyard at Kilbarrack, apparently built on sand, dates from 1654, but it lies on the site of the twelfth or thirteenth century chapel of Mone, or the Abbey of Kilbarrack, which was situated on bog or marsh. The name Kilbarrack is derived from the church of Berach, with St. Berach's well north of the church (reputedly the church was founded in the sixth century). A fee, most likely in money or fish, was paid by mariners up until the time of the reformation in 1538 (Igoe, V., 2001, *Dublin Burial Grounds and Graveyards*, Dublin, Wolfhound Press).

On Archbishop Allan (Burdy, S., 1817, *The History of Ireland, from the Earliest Ages to the Union*, Edinburgh, Duncan Stevenson and Company).

Deliberate beaching was by no means a historical impossibility. In 1813, for example, the captain of *The Brothers* from Lisbon deliberately shored his fruit-laden vessel on the Bull by cutting the main mast and using only the foremast in a dreadful tempest (Anon., 1813, September 7, *Belfast Newsletter*, p. 3).

A ship with artillery and munitions was also lost on the Dublin bar in 1562, as was another unnamed ship in 1574 – a Captain Piers lost his plate and staff (Brady, K., 2008, *Shipwreck Inventory of Ireland*, Dublin, Stationery Office).

On Plumptre (Scale, Bernard and Richards, William, 1765, *Directions for Navigating into the Bay of Dublin from Wicklow Head and from Balbriggen*, Dublin, S. Powell and Son).

A flag/ensign on the lighthouse indicated when it was safe to enter during the day, a lanthorn by night (Scale, Bernard and Richards, William, 1765).

The fragility of human technology stretches into prehistory: in 1935, an ancient dugout canoe was found in the sandpits near Sutton.

Until recently only 25 shipwrecks are associated with the Bull sands in local history: The mail packet *The William* (1690), *Friendship* (1726), *Hope* (1727), *Hannel and Betty* (1755), *Sally* (1767), *Nancy* (1769), *Durly* (1770), *Graneda* (1772), *Anthony* (1773), *Elizabeth* (1774), *Clyde* (1790), *Young Murray* (1791), *Active Cargo Ship* (1798), *Penguin* (1799 – all 65 hands lost), *Dolphin* (1799), *Ceres* (1814 – Sutton Sound), *Ontario* (1817), *Prince of Wales* (1819), *Atlantic* (1821), *Ellen* (1825), *Defiance* (1825), *Fame* (1826), *Hampton* (1874), *Geo. H. Oulton* (1881), *Dispatch* (1886), *Charles Bal* (1888), and the *Antelope* (1950) – on whose decks the historian Lynch stood on the day after it beached (Lynch, V., 2007, *No Thoroughfare on the Tram Road*, Dublin, Johnswood Press).

However, the definitive source, *Brady's Shipwreck Inventory of Ireland*, now indicates 175 shipwrecks, relating to a narrowly defined Bull area alone, and not including the *Martha Grace* (1860), *Joanna Eliza* (1885) and *Otway* (1867). We can also add the brigantine *Harmony* in 1886 (Anon., 1866, September 22, *The Freeman's Journal*, p. 3), *The Katy* (Knowles, 1970) and other vessels mentioned in this book.

Similarly, in 1762 we find reports of two ships lost, whose names were unknown (Anon., 1762, March 23, *Belfast Newsletter*, p. 2); ditto for one wreck on North Bull that washed up at Annesley Bridge, name unknown (Anon., 1804, November 9, *Belfast Newsletter*, p. 2). Brady puts the entire number of unknowns at 76. And of course not everything wrecked would have been reported lost.

At times it is also unclear if some boats such as the barque *Barbara*, which had its cargo removed after coming ashore on the North Bull, were put back to sea (Anon., 1863, November 6, *Freeman's Journal*, p. 2); ditto for the barque *Premier*, which came ashore at the Sutton end of the Bull in 1863 (Anon., 1863, November 5, *Freeman's Journal*, p. 3). What became of the *Ajax*, which came ashore in 1862 in a perfect hurricane (Anon., 1862, January 23, *Freeman's Journal*, p. 3)?

Occasionally, mammals are found dead on the Bull. In 2004, for example, a male porpoise was found decomposing on the strand by the Irish Coast Guard (Philpott, E., Wall, D. and Rogan, E., 2007, 'Records from the Irish Whale and Dolphin Group for 2004', *The Irish Naturalists' Journal*, 28(9), 379-385).

On hacked porpoises (Anon., 1932, July 24, 'Weather Lore', *Sunday Independent*, p. 4, citing 'A Diary of the Weather and Winds for 19 years, 1716-1734).

Green-finned oysters and herring with vivid green backs were also reported in the region.

On shark rarity (Anon., 1846, July 31, *Freeman's Journal*, p. 3).

The remaining limb of the boy's skeleton had on a boot and stocking. Clothing was intact on the body. He was five to six months in the water. He was interred unidentified (Anon., 1881, November 18, *Freeman's Journal*, p. 2).

The pilot whale's fate was somewhat more dignified than events of 600 years earlier. In 1331, when a school of 'Thurlehydes' (whales) became stranded near Ringsend – during a famine – they were promptly eaten.

In 1995, the Natural History Museum acquired one bobtail squid (*Sepiola atlantica (d'orb)*). Eugen O Mahony found it at Sutton Creek.

On the shore: the short-snouted seahorse (*Hippocampus antiquorum* and *H. brevirostris Cuv* (Jeffrey, 1977)).

On triggerfish (Quigley, D.T.G., 1987, 'First record of the triggerfish balistes carolinensis (Gmelin, 1789) from Co. Dublin, and a further record from Co. Cork', *The Irish Naturalists' Journal*, 22(5), 207).

4

Captain Bligh

In the lore of the city, the North Bull Wall was built by Captain William Bligh. This somewhat overstates his contributions, but it is hardly surprising. In 1789, Bligh had already achieved a stellar if inglorious fame after his crew cast him adrift from his ship the *Bounty*. And even in Dublin it is the *Mutiny on the Bounty*, not the wall, which mostly secures his fame to this day. Accompanying this fame was a certain amount of infamy. Bligh's biographer describes his teeth as marlin spikes, his hair as rope, and that any man who disobeyed his 'mad ruthless orders' seldom lived to do it twice. Others describe him as a puritanical sadist.

The North Bull Wall was a vast engineering project, as impressive as any in Europe at that time (Dublin was a major European city), and numerous engineers were actually involved. Their various roles are tangled and complex. At one level, the construction of the North Wall took place under Inspector of Works George Halpin alongside the contributions of Francis Giles and build engineer captain Daniel Corneill. At another level, engineering communications from multiple authors had been flying across the city in various

17

forms from 1801 to 1805. So there were various consultations with other contemporaries such as Captain Whidbey and Thomas Telford.

In 1800, Bligh himself had noted in a survey of Dublin Bay that the Liffey's mouth was blocked with sand and that very few ships could find a place to lie afloat at low water. Accompanying these self-evident observations, Bligh had more usefully taken crucial water depth measurements and surveyed the site. He noted a permanent dry patch and three wrecks. And either indirectly or directly, Bligh's knowledge appears to have gained him at least some say in the wall's construction, along with some powerful family connections.

In 1814, the Ballast Board surveyed the site, and drew up plans and estimates that found their way via government to the Board of Inland Navigation. Halpin notes visits to the construction site by the 'directors general of inland navigation', such as John Rennie, Thomas Hyde Page and Captain Bligh, or 'the most eminent scientific and practical men of that day'. Halpin refers to Bligh as a talented officer who acquired a thorough knowledge of the bay. However, the design of the breakwater appears to have actually originated in earlier proposals by William Chapman around 1786. Bligh's own proposal for a wall running almost parallel to the south wall was *rejected*. In fact, one dismissive tract, weighing up the merits of all the proposals, excuses him on the grounds that 'engineering was not the study of his life'.

Little is remembered about the many convict labourers who actually built the wall. Instead, Bligh's name – or a hazy sense of his fame, infamy and association with the wall – is remembered fondly. Indeed, as the nineteenth century and the wall's many engineers passed into history, only Bligh's name remained in the memory of Dubliners.

Captain Bligh – Notes

On Bligh's biographer (Anon., 1963, January 19, 'Bligh on the Bull Island', *Irish Press*, p. 6).

Bligh as a sadist (McIntyre, 1987).

There may have been plans to extend the Bull Wall further. In 1829, it was noted that the building had been halted to judge if the 'experiment will succeed' (Smith, E., 1829, *The Kaleidoscope: or, Literary and Scientific Mirror, Vol 4*, Liverpool, E. Smith, p. 110).

On Bligh's family connections (Flood, D.T., 1975, *Dublin Historical Record*, Vol. 28, No. 4, pp. 142-153).

A plan for the harbour published by Rennie was rejected. His design did include a North Bull Wall-like edifice, but with an eastwards kink at the end (Civis, Pseud., 1804, *A Letter Addressed to His Excellency, Philip, Earl of Hardwicke, Lord Lieutenant of Ireland, Upon the Improvement of the Harbour of Dublin*, Dublin, William Watson).

On eminent men (Anon., 1836, *Parliamentary Papers, House of Commons and Command*, Vol. 24, London, H.M. Stationery Office).

On Chapman (De Courcy, 1996).

Contributions by two members of the Ballast Board, Maquay and Crosthwaite, were also made in 1801 (Corry, G., 1970, 'The Dublin bar: The obstacle to the improvement of the port of Dublin', *Dublin Historical Record*, 23(4), pp. 137-152).

Thomas Hyde Page also approved of a wall from the North Lotts running towards the North Bull sands in 1801, which had earlier been suggested by the commissioners of navigation but which didn't get built (Page, T.H., 1801, *Reports Relative to Dublin Harbour and Adjacent Coast*, Dublin).

The anonymous tract also argues that Bligh had only three months' experience of the bay in contrast to fifty years by some of the others (Civis, Pseud., 1804).

On convicts (McIntyre, 1987).

5

A Known Art

With the building of the North Bull Wall, it is not clear if there was any official intention to accelerate the growth of the Bull as an island. But reclamation was a known art that had long been used extensively in the city of Dublin. The city was confident it could take what it wanted from the sea – it was just a matter of cost. Indeed, because of this confidence, turning some of Dublin's sand bars into an island had already been mooted in 1792 by the highly regarded engineer Sir Thomas Hyde Page. This imaginary island, directly south of the North Bull, shows up on a map on an anonymous pamphlet published in 1804.

Moreover, in 1812, immediately prior to the wall's construction, when plans were already afoot to build the wall, Edward Wakefield noted that in a few years there would be pastures, or at least rabbit warrens, on the North Bull, and that this process could be accelerated. Similarly, Plumptre in 1814 suggested that if the Irish were more *industrious*, a vast tract of the North Bull might be rescued from the water and made into cultivatable land. For all that, the stated aims of the wall's construction appear to have been merely to facilitate shipping and to save lives. Perhaps given the projected costs, plans any more grandiose may have sunk the project.

Over the years, the odd attempt has been made to re-count the natural history of the island's 'reclamation'. In 1948, for example, the marram grass on 'Dublin's pleasure island' was thought to have given way to a fine variety of red fescue, 'which soon covered the island', and was thought ideal for golf. Others would note the accumulation of sand from clock-wise currents in the bay. More scientific accounts emerged in the 1970s.

Salt-tolerant plants such as saltwort and magenta flow-ered sea rocket possibly accumulated on small hummocks of dry sand and seaweed lying on Sand Island or the nearby mudflats. These fragile plants would have accumulated sand in their roots and provided a higher embryonic platform for couchgrass and scutchgrass, whose creeping stems and roots could rapidly anchor a nascent dune. Sand again could accu-mulate and make way for other grass species such as marram. But for all that, nature's actual reclamation process around 1820 is not clear. Indeed, speculation remains perilous. Some species of grass – such as lyme grass – were seemingly only first noted in 1892. The invasive spartina was introduced by humans.

A Known Art – Notes

On the imaginary island (Civis, Pseud., 1804).

On pastures (Wakefield, E., 1812, *An Account of Ireland, Statistical and Political*, London, Longman, Hurst, Rees, Orme and Brown).

A plan in the 1870s to discharge mud and sweet sweepings in 'trap bottom boats' onto the North Bull, and so form acres of 'made land', was rejected twice (Anon., 1872, March 2, *The Nation*, p. 8).

'Dublin's pleasure island' was also considered ideal for golf fairways (Anon., 1948, September 12, 'Dublin's Pleasure Island Rose from the Sea', *Sunday Independent*, p. 6).

On clockwise currents and sediment (Corry, G., 1970, 'The Dublin bar: The obstacle to the improvement of the port of Dublin', *Dublin Historical Record*, 23(4), pp. 137-152; Harris, C.R., 1980, *Journal of Earth Sciences*, 3(1), 41-52).

The island's formation process is based on Jeffrey (1977). Old by modern science's standards, but explicitly related to the Bull itself.

On lyme grass (McArdle, D., 1892, 'Clematis vitabla, L., on the North Bull, Dollymount, Co. Dublin', *The Irish Naturalist*, 1(6), p. 125).

6

The Island the Sea Swallowed

Just as Bull Island was appearing the sea swallowed a nearby westerly island – Clontarf Island. This low lying island lay south of an area of deep water anchorage known as the Clontarf Pool, which merged with the estuary of the Ballybough River (now the Tolka River). From 1666, 'pesthouses' were built on the island to contain plague from London and elsewhere. In 1729, passing naturalist Caleb Trelkeld noted the presence of the yellow poppy. Its yellow clay banks were covered in shells and seapink. A natural habitat for birds, the island also had a popular bathing pool with a ferry service in the 1840s from the city's East Wall road. On the southern end perched a small wooden residence, 'island house', visible as early as 1745 in an engraving by George King. This was famously and *ominously* swept away with two so-called descendants of Cromwell in an October storm in 1844. The island was beautifully sketched by Alex Williams R.H.A in 1878; the drawing shows boats, birds, a gangplank and a picturesque log cabin – though there were probably two cabins used by fishermen. To the south of the island was a body of water known as the Salmon Poole.

Rocque's map of 1753 clearly charts the island. And in 1881, it was still being mapped by Gilmore. But by the late 1880s, Clontarf Island had disappeared into the sea. The reason for the disappearance of the island is clear. The building of the south wall and other parts of Dublin (such as the Alexandra Basin within the city port) involved catastrophic but legal quarrying of the island's gravel. Compounding the quarrying, Dubliners had also helped themselves to the muddy sands of the island for uses such as fertilizer. Accompanying such quarrying was the apparent attitude that the island was merely an expendable resource. In 1883, the Port and Docks Board prohibited the removal of sand from the island – unless you paid. By the turn of the twentieth century Clontarf Island was barely visible at low tide; its population of birds displaced. Some flat stones and the remains of wooden structures at its western end were noted in 1912. Even then, barges scraped away anything left. It was soon forgotten. Things physically destroyed often are.

The Island the Sea Swallowed – Notes

Clontarf Island is also referenced as 'Cromwell's Island' (McIntyre, 1987). De Courcy shows the differences in various representations of Clontarf Island (De Courcy, 1996).

The estimated size of Clontarf Island was about 400 yards by 40 yards and 16 feet high. To its east Rocque's map labels the sands 'Browns Patch'. Ballybough is an area just outside the city and contiguous with Fairview, which itself extends along the coast into Clontarf.

In 1538, the Priory of Kilmainham granted a lease of the lands of Clontarf with Clontarf Island to Mathew King, in whose family it remained until the Commonwealth. It was later confiscated and given to John Blackwell, a friend of the protector [Oliver Cromwell], from whom it passed into possession of the Vernon family (Joyce, Weston St. John, 1912, *The Neighbourhood of Dublin*, Dublin, M.H. Gill & Son). Blackwell sold it to John Vernon in 1660, together with rights to anchorage, fisheries, creeks, sands and seashore wrecks (Anon., 1920, February 3, *Freeman's Journal*, p. 5). One source suggests the island was used to quarantine victims of the 1650 plague and that in 1600 Kilmainham Priory also granted the island to Sir Geoffery Fenton (Bown, B.P., 1950, 'The north strand', *Dublin Historical Record*, 11(2), pp. 1-57). Elswhere, De Courcy indicates the 'pesthouses' were built in 1666 to quarantine passengers, following concern over plague in London. A quarantine sloop is also visible in the Poolbeg on Rocque's map (De Courcy, 1996).

A 1728 map by Charles Brooking labels the island, the pool and the mainland as 'Clandaf'. The Down Survey mapping of 1658 appears to label it as '[c?]lantaf isle'.

On yellow poppy (Threlkeld, C., 1729, *Synopsis Stirpium, Hibernicarum Alphabetice Dispositarum*, Dublin, S. Powell). Trelkeld's spelling is 'Clantarff'.

On seapink (Williams, A., 1908, *The Irish Naturalist*. Vol. 17, No. 9, September, pp. 165-170).

A stone curlew was shot on Clontarf Island in 1849 (Kinahan, in Proc. Dublin Univ. Zool. Assocn., 25th November 1854). Several pairs of Kentish plover also appear to have nested here during the winter of 1852 (Ussher, R.J. and Warren, R., 1900, *The birds of Ireland: An account of the distribution, migrations and habits of birds as observed in Ireland, with all additions to the Irish list*, London, Gurney and Jackson). But for extensive details on birds see Williams, A. (1908).

A 1673 map in the UK National Maritime museum also shows a settlement marked on Clontarf Island (McGettigan, D., 2013, *The Battle of Clontarf*, Dublin, Four Courts

Press); George King's engraving was itself inspired by a work by William Jones (c.f. NGI.10007).

On Cromwell's non-descendants (McIntyre, 1987).

Publican Christopher Cromwell and his son were on the island. The lights on the cabin went out at 10.00 pm on October 9th. The storm destroyed the house, bathing shelters and wooden changing huts. Their bodies washed up on the railway embankment the next day (Lynch, 2007).

Sketch of the island (Williams, A., 1908).

South of the Salmon Poole existed a body of water on the South Bull known as 'Cock Lake' (Greenville's map, 1686; Moore, N., 2008, *Dublin Docklands Reinvented*, Dublin, Four Courts Press).

Bligh's map of 1800 shows 'Clontarf Island' as quite small; for clarification see (Flood, D. T., 1975, *Dublin Historical Record*, Vol. 28, No. 4, pp. 142-153).

Clontarf Island appears in Gilmore's 1881 'Chart of Dublin Bar' (Moore, N., 2008, *Dublin Docklands Reinvented*, Dublin, Four Courts Press).

The birds from Clontarf Island and the considerably reduced South Bull/Shelly Bank moved to the North Bull (Kennedy, P.G., 1935, 'Bird Life on the North Bull', *The Irish Naturalists Journal*, 5(7), 165-168). Kennedy was a noted ornithologist with an international reputation. He was one of a group of enthusiasts whose work led to the establishment of the country's three bird sanctuaries. He died in 1967 (Anon., 1967, March 13, *Irish Press*, p. 4).

A perhaps apocryphal tale speaks of a boat taking a flying leap in one particular storm (Anon., 1836, *Minutes of Evidence Taken Before the Committee on the Dublin and Drogheda Railway and Report*, London, Cox and Sons).

A 1717 map by Bolton shows the strand north of the island described as 'quarry resserv'd in common for the work' (De Courcy, 1996).

Howth limestone was also used as fertilizer (c.f. Drummond's Clontarf) as was seaweed (Knowles, F., 1970, *Old Clontarf*, p. 8); special shipways to the seashore existed to facilitate farmers around Clontarf in their harvesting of seaweed (McIntyre, 1987).

Quarrying may have been partially responsible for the disappearance of certain promontories on the Clontarf coast such as 'Cockle point', 'Cold harbour' and 'The Furlong' (McIntyre, 1987). Much of the shingle and boulders near Clontarf Strand and the area projecting spit from the Sheds known as Clontarf Head may also have been removed over the years (De Courcy, 1996).

On the remains of the island (Joyce, Weston St. John, 1912; Williams, A., 1908).

7

Vikings: The Raven's Banner

As mentioned earlier, the story of Bull Island is overshad-owed by the Battle of Clontarf – a bloody encounter in 1014 between a coagulation of Vikings Norse/Danes/Leinster-men and the army of Irish high king Brian Bóru. The 10,000 or so warriors met somewhere north of the Tolka and south of Howth, on a plain known as *Mag na Ealta*.

The *Annals of Lough Cé* tell us that Brian beached/set up/made (*Gabhair*) a 'longphort' at Clontarf. The area surround-ing the Clontarf Pool, including the now absent promontory known as the furlong (an inversion of longphort?), would have made a highly plausible site for this – indeed, historically it has consistently been seen and used as a natural harbour (with good fresh water supplies). In 1014, even in a time of limited military strategy, it may have served as a location with possible offensive and defensive uses. If Brian controlled this 'longport', his attackers may have preferred to land a slight distance away, such as on the Bull sands coastal area.

Either way, when the routed forces under the raven banner fled, some portion of them made for the sea, where a subse-quent shore massacre and drownings seem to have occurred.

It is not clear if the Bull sands were in fact present or absent in 1014, but the Earl of Orkney, Jarl Sigurd – before he fell – was advised to make for an area known as *Dumazbakki*, variously translatable as 'mound-bank', 'sand dune' or 'sand bank'. In 1910, E.A. Hogan argued the location to be 'a long and remarkable sandbank at Clontarf opposite Dollymount' (deriving from the old Irish word for sandbank, *dumach*, a view supported by Taylor in 1958. It is by no means inconceivable then that this hypothesised sandbank of 1014, where the fleet may have been on or very close to, was that which later became known as the North Bull sands. In any case, the 30 plus vessels were supposedly taken by a high tide (or torched) and unavailable for use.

That said, though large sand dunes have been recorded at Clontarf, dunes are also historically known to have existed closer to Dublin, where an attacking fleet may also have landed. *Dumazbakki* might actually mean 'grave hill', and the text may simply be an interpolation rendering the whole idea redundant. A large school of thought also moves the attempt at flight and massacre nearer to a supposed weir at Ballybough, closer to Dublin. This does not rule out the possibility of some occurrences near the North Bull sands, but it does make any role for them appear less significant.

All the same, a Viking sword/grave was dug up nearly opposite the present Bull Wall at Danesfield House, and some historians believe the weir may have been closer to Clontarf. Local lore also sources at least some of the battle to Conquer Hill, just west of Dollymount (adjacent to Bull Island), which again could suggest a nearby landing site. Furthermore, even if this was not the landing/escape site, it seems likely that some Danes would have considered an escape north towards

Howth. When your life is at stake, the shore in either direction along the sands is as good a way to escape as any (if not for the tide).

Complicating any analysis is a glorious amount of myth surrounding the events of 1014. During the battle, for example, a greenish dog-like animal rose from the sea to protect the body of King Tadhg Ua Ceallaigh. Other popular myths and supernatural occurrences include *bean sídhe* visitations and prophecy, flying swords, attacks by ravens, use of dragon blood and blood rain.

But myth aside, the 'Vikings' did plunder nearby Lambay in 797 AD and over-wintered in Dublin from as early as 842 AD onwards, so it seems uncontroversial to assert that Norse, Danes etc. visited the Bull area at some point. Excavations of their Dublin settlement at Wood Quay also revealed an impressive variety of bird remains now common to Howth and the Bull sands. But all that can be said for certain is that there is *no direct evidence* to support an association of the North Bull sands (if they even existed) with the 'Vikings' of 1014 *per se*.

The only thing that even briefly threatened to overshadow Clontarf's famous association with 1014 was a 'monster meeting' that Daniel O'Connell planned there for October 1843. A letter to the editor of the *Freeman's Journal* in September of the same year suggested it be held on 'an island' called the 'North Bull', because it could accommodate up to 700,000 people. Nothing came to pass; the assembly was proscribed by British Prime minister Robert Peel – backed up with troops and warships – in an atmosphere of acute political tension.

The fact that the island later had enough merit to be made a UNESCO biosphere does not even make a splash in Irish history books; in Ireland, as elsewhere, political history has tended to supersede ecological history. And yet prior to the wall's construction many different species were poised for territorial advances and invasions.

Vikings: The Raven's Banner – Notes

Howth is seemingly derived from the Norse *Hofuth*, meaning head or promontory; the Norse-sounding *Clumtorp* was used for Clontarf in the 1170s when the Knights Templar were granted rights (Lennon, Colm, 2012, 'The medieval manor of Clontarf, 1171-1540', in S. Duffy (ed.), *Medieval Dublin XII*, Dublin, Four Courts Press).

Mag n-elta (plain of flocks), also called *Senmag n-elta*, is the territory between Dublin and Howth. Todd, extracting from the *Annals of the Four Masters* and other manuscripts, notes that Clontarf was anciently called *Sen Magh-nEalta Edair*, or old plain of the flocks of Edair (Todd, J.H., 1867, *The War of the Gaedhil with the Gaill*, London, Longmans, Green, Reader and Dyer).

In some accounts, *Cath Coradh Cluana tarbh/Cat Corad Cluan tarb*, is used to refer to the battle and is traditionally translated as the battle of the fishing weir of Clontarf, the weir supposedly being near the Ballybough bridge, where a weir at the Tolka once may have been. However, looking at early maps we can see that the Tolka river estuary and its weir could easily have stretched at least as far as Clontarf Island in 1014. Small rivers also existed along the Clontarf coast and possibly another weir did as well.

It is by no means certain that all of Brian's enemies had shallow-bottomed boats. If there were deep-bottomed boats then the Clontarf Pool increases in importance as a possible harbour.

On *Dumazbakki* (Taylor, A.B., 1958, 'Dumazbakki: An Irish place name in old Norse form'. *The Journal of the Royal Society of Antiquaries of Ireland*, 88(2), 111-114).

Rocque's map of 1756 shows a series of dry islands along the whole northern coast as far as the Sheds which may have been dunes, but then again may have been oyster beds.

An ornamented Viking pin was also found buried in Clontarf. It was declared Scandinavian and dated to the ninth century (Milligan, S.F., 1906, March 31, *The Journal of the Royal Society of Antiquaries of Ireland*. Fifth Series, Vol. 36, No. 1, [Fifth Series, Vol. 16] , p. 87).

Conquer Hill's etymology could lie in the Irish for 'rabbit warren' (*coinicear*) or 'the heron's head' (*ceann-cor*), which perhaps refers to a settlement of displaced fishermen from the Sheds (McIntyre, 1987). See discussion elsewhere in the book for more.

On the battle of Clontarf (Duffy, Seán, 2013, *Brian Boru and the Battle of Clontarf*, Dublin, Gill & Macmillan).

Speculatively, the green of the mythical greenish sea dog may have been a mistranslation of the Irish *glas* and in fact referenced grey. This would make the mythical creature something like a dolphin or porpoise, which could be argued to have a certain morphological similarity to the Irish wolfhound.

On *bean sídhe* (Hore, H. and Mac Ritchie, D., 1895, 'Origin of the Irish superstitions regarding banshees and fairies', *The Journal of the Royal Society of Antiquaries of Ireland*, 5(2), pp. 115-129).

On bloodrain (Tatlock, J., 1914, 'Some Mediaeval Cases of Blood Rain, *Classical Philology*, 9(4), 442-447).

The bird bone fragments from Viking settlements in Dublin include the following seen on Bull Island in 2012: the buzzard, crow, oystercatcher, herring gull, cormorant, kittiwake, gannet, curlew, bar-tailed godwit, guillemot, duck, red-throated diver, shag, marsh harrier, raven, peregrine, swan, goose and rook (D'Arcy, G., 1999, *Ireland's Lost Birds*, Dublin, Four Courts Press; for the 2012 list see Cooney, Tom, 2012, *North Bull Island Birds*, www.bullislandbirds.com). The white eagle, osprey and kite were also found but were not present in 2012.

On a monster meeting on the Bull (Anon., 1843, September 9, 'To the editor of the Freeman', *Freeman's Journal*, p. 3). The favoured location for Daniel O'Connell's monster meeting was on the shore at Conquer hill (De Courcy, 1996).

8

The Botanists

In 1726, Caleb Threlkeld wrote a short treatise on native Irish plants, especially those growing spontaneously in the vicinity of Dublin. On the way side leading to 'Clantarf' he noted 'musked cranesbill', and in the hedges, privet. He noted 'hemp leafed' dead nettle near 'Clantarff wood' and nearby wild daffodil. But it is seaward where things get more interesting. Threlkeld noted the presence of ladies finger on 'the dry hillocks' near the sea on the north side of the bay of Dublin. On the dry banks facing nearby Poolbeg – hence possibly Sand Island – he found 'cranesbill without scent' – the lack of odour he attributed to soil differences.

He found sea spurge on the shore parallel to the Bull sands between 'Warren house' and Raheny; and oyster green or sea lettuce on the shore rocks. Threlkeld also notes that Dubliners were in the habit of chewing dried-out seaweed, *dillisk*, like a tobacco, while an appendix by Dr. Thomas Molyneux (physician to the state) further notes the presence of broad leaved horn wrack. Molyneux states that it was gathered by his wife on the strand beyond Clontarf on 16 March 1694 – though he does not say for what purpose.

A little later, in 1794, Walter Wade (who successfully petitioned parliament for a public botanic garden) recorded
sea holly, perfoliate yellow wort, corn mouse ear chickweed,
pimpernel rose, yellow horned poppy and hemlock cranes
bill. Charting rarities in 1804, Wade also noted the 'mouse ear
pearl work'. This flowered in July on the sandy shore between
Clontarf and Howth. Between these two points, he also noted
the round fruited rush, goose corn, moss rush, little bulbous
rush, and great sharp rush. Between Clontarf and the Warren house (near Kilbarrack) he noted portland spurge and
between 'The Sheds' (a fishing village where fish was once
cured) and the old mill ground of Raheny he noted yellow
mountain pansy. Before there was ever a botanical presence
on the island then, the ancestors of the plants were seemingly
waiting and biding their time on the nearby shore.

The Botanists – Notes

Threlkeld interchangeably supplied Irish, Latin and English names in his writing.

As noted elsewhere, the orthography of Clontarf var-
ies. The 1589 Ortelius map reads 'Clontarfe' (which along
with Hothe was the only significant landmark north of the
shore).

Ladies finger, i.e. kidney vetch.

The 'dry bank' on the Bull, mapped in 1804, might cor-
respond to the dry banks facing Poolbeg mapped by
Threlkeld, but we don't know if it existed this early (Civis,
Pseud., 1804).

Sea lettuce, *Lichen marinus*, which the poor of Northumberland added to their soup, was found to be over three feet long at Sutton Creek by E.A. Lotts in 1907.

Threlkeld notes: sea wrack, sea weed with skinny horns, *fucus–membranaceus-ceranoides*. Elsewhere in the book our hero also collects moss growing on a dead man's skull, and complains that the Oaks of Kildare have been destroyed through mismanagement.

On Wade's records (Wade, Walter, 1794, *Catalogus Systematicus Plantarum Indigenarum in Comiatut Dublinensi*, Dublin, Gul Sleator). Wade was Professor and Lecturer of Botany to the Dublin Society.

Mouse ear pearl, *Sagina ceratoides*; portland spurge, *Euphorbia portlandica*.

On Wade's later findings (Wade, W., 1804, *Plantae Rariores in Hibernia Inventae Or, Habitats of Smoe Plants, Rather Scarce and Valuable*, Graisberry and Campbell).

9

Dead Leg Beats Sprained Ankle

In early April 2013, I went down to the beach with my son Hugh, age 6, who loves books and can't stop talking. We joined the local volunteers cleaning up the beach. Soon we were winding through the marshland behind the dunes picking up tinfoil, paper, half a tennis ball and other human oddities.

Somehow, over the next hour, we made our way into the heart of a marshy labyrinth, swollen from months of unseasonal rain. Hugh was getting tired, hungry and missing his mum, Maebh. I did not want to take him the whole way back. Jumping a small stream – with Hugh on my shoulder – looked like a nice short cut. As I landed I sprained my ankle quite badly; walking was impossible. To make matters funnier, we had jumped on to a small island; I would need an adult to bear my weight and help me back across the marsh water.

We made some phone calls. Unable to locate us, a friend then informed some nearby Gardaí. The Gardaí however could not come immediately because one of the other clean-up volunteers had seemingly found a dead leg. The possibility of a leg being found seemed eminently plausible to me. In 1994, the body of a retired seaman buried eight miles out to sea washed up opposite the island's interpretative centre. The legs beneath the knees and arms beneath the elbows were missing. The torso was only identifiable by tattoo. So the Gardaí were left to do their job, while I tried to figure out my coordinates and better describe our location.

In the end I was rescued by a local man. He had been out walking two beautiful dogs, and gracefully waded across the water to rescue both myself and Hugh. As it turned out I had not sprained my ankle – I had broken it. And the Gardaí hadn't found a dead leg – they had found a shotgun wrapped in old jeans.

Sometimes the sea gifts only nightmares. On April 28, 2013, the body of a man was washed up on the beach. A morning walker found him. He appeared to be in his late twenties. Though the Gardaí had not yet identified him, they were not treating the death as suspicious. As you might have guessed by now, such a find has never been that unusual on this island. That said, D.A. Chart's 1906 comment that the sand beaches where children paddle were strewn with corpses in summer was probably hyperbole.

When a bird is washed up, the ornithologists on the island call it a tideline corpse. Ravens have been known to feed on them.

Dead Leg Beats Sprained Ankle – Notes

The torso with the tattoo (Anon., 1994, February 8, *The Irish Times*).

On beach strewn with corpses (Anon., 1906, by D.A. Chart, M.A. *Irish Independent*, p. 4).

Ravens feeding on tideline corpse (Kennedy, 1935).

10

The Wooden Bridge

One way to access the island is via a long, narrow wooden bridge which crosses water or mud flats, depending on the vagaries of the tide. Coming out along the north coast from the city centre as far as Clontarf, it's hard to miss. Cars can rumble slowly across it, but only in single file. At each side, a separate part of the bridge is reserved for cyclists and pedestrians. The planks sing hollow as you step on them. In their imagination, children fall through the gaps and disappear. From dusk to dawn, a species of bat, the *Leisler Bat* (also known as the hairy-armed bat), swoops near the bridge's murky lights looking for insects.

The bridge has a minor cameo role in Joyce's *Portrait of an Artist*, as his hero Stephen Daedalus crosses on to Bull Island:

> He turned seaward from the road at Dollymount
> and as he passed on to the thin wooden bridge he
> felt the planks shaking with the tramp of heavily
> shod feet. A squad of Christian brothers was on its
> way back from the Bull and had begun to pass, two
> by two, across the bridge. Soon the whole bridge
> was trembling and resounding.

Joyce was probably referring here to an occurrence of what was elsewhere described as 'a Lilliputian army' of 700 boys from the distant Artane Industrial School. Such boys were marched over the bridge by the Christian Brothers with military discipline and a trumpet. They were taken along the Bull Wall to bathe – not swim. Now, in more liberated summers, bikini-clad sirens and their lovers jump from the railings into the high tide. Sometimes they even jump into lower tides, oblivious of rocks and blissfully unaware that the body of the suicidal John M. Bird was once found floating under the bridge – with his hard felt hat crushed down over his eyes.

Aside from being two sides of the coin that is repression and liberation, both these generations share a belief in immortality. The first paid additional emphasis to the spirit. The second pays greater homage to youth. The environment also plays second fiddle to both; for many Christians it is expendable, perhaps even necessarily so. For many of the lovers it can probably be fixed tomorrow. This belief is not their fault. Their parent's faith is progress.

The present bridge is not the original. This one was built in 1907 and restored in 2008. But the wooden stumps of the original, built around 1819, can still be seen at low tide. The bridge was originally wide enough for horse-drawn carriages, but for reasons unknown was narrowed to a footbridge – anything wider being forced to ford the creek. Strictly speaking, the purpose of the bridge was *not* to allow people to flow over it (or jump from it). Instead, it was to allow useful bay tides around the back of the Bull to flow *under* it undisturbed; the flow at the back of the island being deemed useful for, among other things, the bay's important flow of 'back water'. This was not to be interfered with – though in the 1960s, as we shall see, the city would do just that.

The bridge leads past a small guard hut and to the 1.7 kilometre-long wall itself. As you set foot on the island the sea is to your right. Dog whelks eat the barnacles and limpets that are found on the seaward bank. The sea sponge known as breadcrumb clings to it. Within the wall are boulders of carboniferous limestone drawn by cart from Clontarf quarries. And sometimes visible in these boulders are fossils of sea lilies that grew on the seafloor some 330 million years ago. At the end of the wall, there is a lower outstretch of rocks known as the breakwater. These were deliberately left low so that the ebb of high tide could prevent nearby currents from becoming too strong. In 1879, *The Alice Wood*, laden with coal, bore down on it in heavy seas. You can still find bits of coal on the sand near the wall.

The Wooden Bridge – Notes

The other access point to the island is by the causeway built midway along the Bull in 1962 – questioning its status as an island.

The Christian Brothers are probably the 'Dolly Monks' later found in *Finnegans Wake.*

On Christian Brothers (Anon., 1880, July 16, *The Irish Times)*; the boys were possibly not allowed to swim for safety reasons. In 1879 one of the boys had ventured so far out of his depth he drowned (Anon., 1879, August 14, *Freeman's Journal*, p. 5).

The use of 'sirens' was found on an Irish fisherman's Internet posting.

On the death of John M. Bird (Anon., 1911, March 18, *The Irish Times*).

A notable parent of progress was the eccentric James A. Abbot, who took his kids down the Liffey on an experimental boat house dubbed by the press as 'Abbot's Ark'. It could quickly convert to and from a raft but was decidedly unseaworthy; it hit the bridge at Dollymount in 1906 (Anon., 1905, August 11, 'Abbot's Ark', *Irish Independent*, p. 7).

In 1875, the bridge was considered shaky and dangerous but the Port and Docks Board did not wish to spend money on its repairs; possibly at this point it was narrowed to a footbridge (Anon., 1875, May 15, *Freeman's Journal*, p. 3). In 1906, the Golf Club and Dollymount Improvement Association again complained that the condition of the bridge was dangerous. The Port and Docks Board decided to rebuild the bridge at its original width (Anon., 1906, March 9, *Irish Independent*, p. 6). In 1923, the bridge was again in need of repair. Heavy military traffic had shaken its timbers (which was claimed to have originally been made from Jarrah wood). Military authorities had also altered the character of the bridge with a sand path to the bridge and tarring. Compensation was being sought from the War Office at the War Claims Commission (Anon., 1923, October 26, *Freeman's Journal*, p. 6).

The bridge used to have an iron gate. In 1908, Mrs Connolly, an employee of the clubhouse, was dashed against the gate with several ribs broken in a high gale (Anon., 1908, February 25, 'Serious Accident at Dollymount', *Freeman's Journal*, p. 1).

In 1881, the bridge is marked as a footbridge on Gilmore's chart of Dublin Bar. In 1892, the Clontarf Township Commissioners requested it be restored to its original length (Anon., 1892, August 1, 'Clontarf Township Commissioners', *The Irish Times*).

The Bull Wall is about 7 metres high and 25 metres wide at its base, stretching 1.75 kilometres to the monument. The breakwater is about 1 kilometre long (Jeffrey, 1977). It is now surfaced with a tar road and concrete footpath, but initially it was topped with square blocks before giving way to a surface of sand and shingle.

Breadcrumb sea sponge – *Halicondria paniciea* (Jeffrey, 1977).

The wall also contains dredged sand and gravel from the bay.

Also visible in the boulders are corals and bryozoa (moss animals).

On the breakwater (Anon., 1836, *Parliamentary Papers, House of Commons and Command, Vol. 24,* London, H.M. Stationery Office).

Over a century after *The Alice* accident, the schooner *Eileen*, built around the 1870s, hit the wall after its captain miscalculated the room necessary to go around the lighthouse perched on the end of the breakwater (Knowles, 1970).

In 1882, the stranded *Electra* also deliberately dumped its cargo of coal overboard (Brady, 2008).

11

Crab Lake, Oysters

To the left of the bridge, as you cross from the mainland, lies an area of water and mudflats known today as Crab Lake. Hence the bridge is sometimes known as 'Crab Lake bridge'. This name extends phonetically from the Irish *Crablough*, which was recognised by Josiah Brown in 1784 as a six-acre stretch of strand near Clontarf. It was also said by Rutty in 1755 to lie opposite to a place called Cold Harbour, which is just north of the wooden bridge and corresponds to today's location. The bridge therefore probably dissected it. Rutty notes in 1772 that crab claws were sometimes used in Dublin to rub on children's sore gums, and since crabs can be found in this location it is tempting to assume crabs were taken from here to market. However, crabs were equally often imported. Furthermore, the Gaelic name probably signifies the presence of boughs by the water's edge rather than crabs. The name may have been derived from an adjacent small inland pool – roughly opposite the Bull Wall – that was also known as Crab Lake, infilled in the 1950s.

In 1755, Rutty noted the presence of tasty 'black cockles' on the North Bull, which were firmer and fatter even in cold weather. The poor made cockle broth; the rich made sauce. Cockles were harvested from April to September (in 1836, they appear to have been harvested predominantly by women). In 1818, the razor fish, whose long narrow shell looks like a razor, was also found hiding in the Bull sands. It was tempted to the surface using salt and brought to market, but was rarely in stock. Mussels on the other hand were not eaten and more often used as bait. They were not eaten much because of not being well understood; they caused great sickness, sometimes leading to death, when incautiously eaten, even if the best ones – the 'Anglice mussel' – were found at Clontarf.

In 1718, Dublin Corporation awarded Alderman Humphrey French the rights to lay down, feed and harvest oysters for 61 years. This privilege was disputed by Clontarf Castle's John Vernon from 1729, at first by seizing, roasting and eating French's oysters, and later in court. The Vernon Estate, or Mary Vernon's tenants, appear to have laid oysters of their own in the area, possibly from as early as 1695. And prior to then Mary Vernon, it was claimed, had already laid down 'salt pipes' on the beach, possibly for supplying salt for curing at the 'herring sheds'. She had rights to and had taken oysters, mussels and cockles from Crablough. She also held written rights to anchorage, wreck and salvage. Though the city did indeed have some rights to the area, John Vernon successfully insisted that they had no rights to the disputed area, which he named – seemingly referencing the area in or around the Bull sands – as Squire's Island.

In any event oyster farming continued. Rocque's map of 1756 shows the oyster beds as a significant landmark directly south of the Sheds and at least the size of Clontarf Island. To their west the map shows Clontarf Pool and Clontarf Island. To the east lay the North Bull sands, separated only by the outflow from local rivers. Oysters were brought annually from Wexford and Arklow to mature before harvesting in May.

Such was the economic focus now associated with the shellfish that a priest in the Clontarf environs would chastise women in his congregation with the charge that, 'such is your depravity, ye wretches, that you would sell your souls for an oyster; nay, even for a cockle'. By 1821, Clontarf oysters were sold all over Dublin by women with famously 'dissonant cries'. Oysters! Curious oysters! Others were sold to France and more often England.

That said, by 1818 (at the latest) the oysters at Clontarf were overharvested, small and gelatinous. In comparison to those in London, quality was iffy. Similarly, Dublin Bay cod was described by Keiran in 1836 as 'nasty'. Nevertheless, oyster farming continued. In 1839, *Thoms Street Directory* shows Clontarf's Thomas Flood as the proprietor of oysters. Irrespective of quality, the oysters retained a certain local cache in Dublin. In 1852, Eliza Cook's journal records that the oysters had been advertised on a placard on a Dublin quay reading 'Erin go Bragh, The real original Clontarf Oysters for sale here'. On the opposite quay, 'Old Established Howth Oysters' could be purchased – under the motto 'Ireland for ever'. At Howth, a natural oyster bed existed off the island Ireland's Eye and the oysters reputedly had distinctly greenish 'fins'.

By 1886 some attempts to preserve oyster beds from their destruction had appeared at the oyster's nursery in Arklow. The close season was extended, and some smaller oysters kept for rebedding. This was not initially to the liking of the fishermen. P. Maher, harbourmaster at Arklow, observed that the fishermen would have happily dredged more oysters in response to the shorter allotted time period. Maher noted that the fishermen 'never for a moment reasoned or thought if they had been allowed to do so they would have destroyed the source from which they draw the means of supporting themselves and their families'.

Nonetheless, Maher somehow seems to have been able to persuade the fishermen with incontrovertible evidence for sustainable harvesting – though of course he did not use that term. By 1886 official records show that Clontarf annually produced a healthy 500 barrels, and Dublin 2,000 barrels.

By the fall of the nineteenth century disaster struck: sewage from the city of Dublin, and more recognisably from Clontarf itself, threatened the oyster industry's survival. Since 1881 it had been recognised that the oysters were no longer thriving well after transplantation. A *Royal Commission on Sewage Report* to the House of Commons noted that Dolly-mount mussels tested for enteritidis – salmonella. Blue point oysters from Clontarf were also tested. Oysters and shellfish, opinion formed, had been sporadically poisoning its citizens.

In 1903, *The Lancet* suggested that typhus also emanated from the septic waters of Clontarf. Surprise was expressed that the farming of oysters had not been discontinued as previously thought. Sir Charles Cameron – scientist, journalist, art critic, historian and Dublin's chief medical officer – notes in his biography that he forced Dublin Corporation to withdraw the licence for the Clontarf oyster beds. Oyster harvesters mostly disappeared (a notable exception being birds such as the oystercatcher). When the area became a special conservation zone, the rights to commercial and hand harvesting were further restricted – though some commercial cockle harvesters continued to flout this law.

Dubliners may have continued to dream of oyster harvesting. But for another reason; it was no longer wise to do so. Not only had sewage filled the bay, generating toxic algae, but toxic sediment from other sources of pollution also now lay at the bottom of the bay, capped by cleaner sediment. When the sea has nightmares, it tosses and churns the sea bed, contaminating its molluscs.

Crab Lake, Oysters – Notes

A historical discussion in the *Freeman's Journal* uses the term *Corriblough* in reference to the lake (Anon., 1920, February 3, *Freeman's Journal*, p. 5).

In 1756, Rocque does not mention cold harbour but does write 'Stone Wharf' close to the supposed Cold Harbour location. The map tentatively suggests that Stone Wharf may just have been an artificial pile of stones; the water now divided by the causeway is labelled 'Raheny Lake'; John Keogh leased a quay at Dollymount in 1782, for bathing and approaching any pleasure boat. It was to be enclosed by iron railing and a stone vase (Gogarty, C., 2013, *From Village to Suburb: The Building of Clontarf Since 1760*, Dublin, Marino Press).

Bligh and Giles both locate Crab Lake away from Cold harbour and closer to the Sheds of Clontarf – and so to the right of the bridge as you cross from the mainland. Giles also notes that the area of strand at Crab Lake, which follows the strand known as the furlong, was known as the 'Back Strand'. A building known as Crab Lake also seems to have existed (Jeffrey, 1977).

The sand to the right of the bridge extending out as far as the end of the wall at low tide was also marked simply 'The Spit' in 1765 (Scale, Bernard and Richards, William, 1765).

Rutty notes that crabs came from as far away as the Isle of Man. The toad or spider crab (*Hyas araneus L.*) was found on the island in 1977 and one from Bull Island is on display in the Natural History Museum of Dublin.

The inland pool known as Crab Lake is visible on early OSI maps; houses were apparently built on the filled-in site.

Common oysters and otter oysters (*Lutraria oblonga*) – typical of those found in Dublin Bay – were found in burial urns with burnt skeleton remains at Palmerstown in 1868 (Frazer, W., 1868, XXXV). On earthen vases found at Palmerstown, one contained human remains, fragments of shell and dog bones (*Proceedings of the Royal Irish Academy*, 10, 336-340).

Cockles were plentiful. Near Haddon Road there was even a slight promontory called Cockle Point (McIntyre, 1987).

On cockle harvesting (Anon., 1836, *Minutes of Evidence Taken Before the Committee on the Dublin and Drogheda Railway and Report*, London, Cox and Sons).

Two female cocklepickers are possibly present in a watercolour by Oliver Mathew Latham sometime after 1860 (c.f. Beached Boats at Clontarf, Dublin; a Group of Figures at National Library).

Picking cockles naturally involved a degree of danger to the naive: an 1830 short story in the *Dublin Literary Gazette* finds a Nurse Susan being advised that some children might gather cockles on the strand at Clontarf, but that 'you must not let them go too far out on the strand lest the tide should surround them and swallow them all up' (Anon., 1830, April 10, 'Pen Sketches by Anthony Outline', *The Dublin Literary Gazette*, 15 , pp. 225-227).

On razor fish (Wartburton, J., Whitelaw, J. and Walsh, R., 1818).

French also had rights to shellfish; as part of the contract he had to supply the Lord Mayor with 10,000 lobsters and each city sheriff with 2,000 (McIntyre, 1987).

The Larceny Act of 1861 would later make stealing oysters from their beds or unlawfully dredging their 'broods' with nets or 'engines' illegal.

In 1705, John Payne was given a lease for 21 years on the oyster beds of Poolbeg that were recorded destroyed in 1715 from building work at Rogerson's Wall above Ringsend. In 1748, the Poolbeg oyster fishery was owned by Bunit and Simpson of Ringsend (De Courcy, 1996).

Salt works were mapped in 1686 by Greenvile Collins (De Courcy, 1996).

On Vernon's dispute (Brown, J., 1784, *Reports of cases, upon appeals and writs of error, Vol. 4*, Dublin, E. Lynch). The Vernon map refers to the Estate of John Vernon Esq, hence one assumes the origin of the name Squire's Island.

To the north of the island, which tails off at Sutton, artificial oyster beds were also laid down. And across the sloppy water, on the southern wall, which ended in the glimmer of the Poolbeg Lighthouse, great brown shelled oysters could be found – often with pearls (Rutty, 1771).

On cockle wretches (Addison, J., 1797, *Interesting anecdotes, memoirs, allegories, essays and poetical fragments*, London).

The Oyster Tavern was also present prior to 1837 on the site of the now demolished Dollymount Hotel (Gogarty, 2013).

On dissonant cries (Wartburton, J., Whitelaw, J. and Walsh, R., 1818).

In 1834, the oyster beds, now numerous and stretching southeast towards the city, were in trouble. Plans for a coastal railroad threatened the oyster beds again. An affidavit of dissent, which claims the beds were there from time immemorial, may have prevented their destruction. J.E. Vernon also petitioned that the enterprise would cause great damage to the port of Clontarf and destroy the sea bathing for a distance of several miles from Dublin.

In 1755, Rutty uses the term 'gelatinous' and claims the oysters were only two inches in diameter, often because they were taken up too soon, so he may be the original source of the claim (but see Wartburton, J., Whitelaw, J. and Walsh, R., 1818).

On 'nasty' cod (Anon., 1836, *Minutes of Evidence Taken Before the Committee on the Dublin and Drogheda Railway and Report*, London, Cox and Sons).

On Maher's comments (House of Commons, 1866, *Reports from Commissioners, Vol. XXVIII*, Great Britain, House of Commons).

In the early 1800s, a water reservoir was built by Weekes on the beach for public use. It is not clear if this was in response to pollution of the local drinking sources.

On Cameron (Frank Hopkins, 2002, *Rare Old Dublin: Heroes, Hawkers & Hoors*, Dublin, Mercier Press, p. 146).

On the subject of pollution: 'Molly Malone may have made a nice living out of Dublin Bay but you wouldn't touch its shellfish with a bargepole today', observed the international co-ordinator of Dublin Bay Environmental Group, Karin Dubsky (Anon., 1990, October 23, *Irish Press*, p. 29).

Clontarf had a lead mine from at least as early as 1497 (De Courcy, 1996).

12

A Pestilent Swamp

In 1790, there were no treatment works in Dublin, for a population of some 210,000. As we have seen this situation would ultimately contribute to the collapse of oyster farming in and around Clontarf. But sewage once also threatened the island itself, via an 1864 plan to handle the city's waste. The smell from the Liffey was offensive; around this time 200 tonnes of raw sewage and industrial waste passed daily through the 'Second City of the Empire'.

The plan in question, by 'Messrs. Barrington and Jeffers' of the Sewage and Land Reclamation Company, envisaged turning the entire island into sewage grounds – supposedly to convert the 'waste lands' of the Bull into productive land. First, they intended to embank the island with a wall. They would then fill the island with 'deodorised' city sewage pumped from nearby Ballybough. Echoing the company's dystopian description of the island, the Dublin Medical Board hailed with satisfaction this plan to reclaim and fertilise 'that desert known as the North Bull.'

One reason why this grandiose dystopian vision came about in the first place was that economic activities in the area had substantially changed. Notably, Clontarf harbour had now silted up. This appears to have been as a direct consequence of building the north and south walls. Furthermore, because direct access to the Liffey and Dublin markets was now easier, this small harbour was no longer economically viable or worth dredging. And the island was not therefore seen as a useful resource for a failed local harbour.

This decline in the importance and viability of commercial shipping activities around Clontarf harbour may also have led to a perceived decline in the ability of its residents to protect their remaining marine interests against this sewage plan. Much of the shell harvesting was undertaken by disempowered women. And already in the 1830s Father Callinan had been granted a 99-year lease to build the church of St. John the Baptist if he cleared a slum of mud huts inhabited by 200 fishing families, which he did. In the 1860s the *Irish Builder* also urged that their subsequent homes – the 'rookeries termed Snugboro' – be razed. Yet aware of a similarly disastrous scheme in Edinburgh, and fearing malaria, a loss of a healthy sea breeze and a property decline of up to 40 per cent, a coalition of local residents rallied against the sewage project and petitioned parliament.

Three important and powerful local landlords also objected. Benjamin Lee Guinness objected that sewage would not produce land but a sea of filth and dirt, a vast lake of dirt – a pestilent swamp. Clontarf's Vernon spoke of a giant sponge of filthy impurity; he would prefer the sea air that God blessed them with than stinking exaltations ('Lay on Macduff,' he threatened). The Earl of Howth argued that the lands actually had been the 'occupation' of gulls and flat fish for centuries.

While in its most grandiose sense Barrington and Jeffers'
scheme did not come to pass, parliamentary plans for sewage
persisted in 1870, and sewage outflow pipes did eventually get
built; they disgorged at the wooden bridge where – as we have
seen – they devastated the oyster beds. Over a century later
Sean Dublin Bay Loftus also observed that the raw sewage
from Ringsend treatment plant was at times still coming on
to the beach. And to this day, heavy rains can cause overflow
of sewage into the bay.

A Pestilent Swamp – Notes

On Second City of the Empire (Anon., 1879, October 2,
Freeman's Journal, p. 2).

The embankment was planned from Sutton to the North
Bull Wall.

Not everyone believed in the idea of deodorising sewage using peat coal. Deodorised sewage, one individual claimed,
was no cure for malaria (Anon., 1869, June 24, *Freeman's
Journal*, p. 4).

On the Dublin Medical Board (Anon., 1864, December 1,
Freeman's Journal, p. 3).

In 1728, there were 'numerous small buildings' in Clontarf;
fishermen's cottages were later described as dilapidated.
A foul smell also existed (presumably the fish) (McIntyre,
1987).

On Father Callinan (McIntyre, 1987).

Despite an austere and difficult lifestyle, fishermen were
known to live to a great age, though by 1835 many poor
in the area subsisted on potatoes, milk and occasionally
bread (McIntyre, 1987).

On a coalition of residents (Anon., 1865, February 2, *The Irish Times*).

On a pestilent swamp (Anon., 1865, February 2, 'The Sewage of Dublin: Meeting in Clontarf', *The Irish Times*, p. 4).

Vernon also mocked the idea of productive lands with a caricatured vision of Jack and the Beanstalk.

The Earl of Howth also acknowledged that the Liffey needed to be purified. But he noted that the suburbs were the children of Dublin – so places such as Balydoyle or Malahide might make a better location.

On sewage (Anon., 1870, November 23, 'In Parliament', *Freeman's Journal*, p. 3).

Sean Loftus changed his name to Sean Dublin Bay Loftus in an attempt to protect the bay.

On raw sewage on the beach (Anon., 1988, January 19, *Irish Press)*.

13

A Consummate Bibliophile

The importance of Clontarf as a harbour is not readily appreciated today. But next to Howth it was one of north Dublin Bay's more useful harbours – and to dismiss it as merely something lesser to Dublin city or other ports underappreciates its historical presence. Readily accessible at high tide, it adjoined the deep water known as the 'Pool of Clontarf', which never went dry, and as such offered badly needed shelter in the bay to boats, large and small.

Trade was not restricted to fishing and was bolstered by the presence of the Knights Templar, who were gifted Clontarf Manor (over 1,100 acres of estate) in the 1170s by Henry II, until their dissolution in 1312 (the Knights Hospitaller of St John subsequently gained the estate and held it until around 1540). In 1358, the port was granted rights to export wheat, along with Dublin and Dalkey. In 1377, the books of a clergyman, which had been shipped to the harbour, were seized by Royal Mandate. In 1395, there was also sufficient traffic for a warrant to be issued to arrest and detain all ships in the water of Clontarf, in an attempt to enforce laws concerning absentee landlords.

Other activities are also well documented. Royal forces are recorded as having landed here in the *Book of Howth*, while in 1416 the Lord Lieutenant John Talbot embarked for England from it. In 1514, there was a bloody encounter between two barques from Dublin and Westchester and two Breton ships, probably commandeered by pirates. In 1527, Clontarf Manor put a four pence anchorage tax on every ship in Clontarf Pool, while during the 1641 rebellion orders were issued for all boats there to be captured or sunk. And arguably the only things that significantly interrupted this activity were periodic outbreaks of disease, most notably the plague of 1348.

The continued importance of the port is visible right up to the north wall's appearance. In 1791, Charles Topham Bowden's *Tour Through Ireland* makes an illustrative and interesting reference to a 'philanthropist' and consummate bibliophile named Christmas Weekes. The intrepid Weekes lived at the Sheds – the location in Clontarf used for curing fish and whose name a local pub retains informally to this day. Weekes had managed to engineer a viaduct from the Sheds to the sands to supply fresh water to any 'vessel frequenting Dublin harbour' that stopped to fill their casks – promptly and without delay. (The sands perpendicularly in front of the Sheds were also known as the 'furlong' and curved along the coast northwards as the back beach; Rocque labels them collectively as 'The North Strand' in 1756.)

The philanthropic Weekes had also managed the entire enterprise without help from parliament, noted the flabbergasted Bowden. Unsurprisingly, the much esteemed Weekes was lauded by Bowden: it was not a trivial undertaking. The task first involved channelling a fresh stream from the environs of the Sheds via the aqueduct to a beach reservoir. The reservoir was equipped with two pumps. In turn, the two pumps appear to have furthered the water along a wharf, projecting about 500 feet into the sea. The wharf also included a platform with seating for people to enjoy sea breezes.

Weekes' wharf was labelled in 1800 on Bligh's map and still retained its 'free of cost' services. But, as stated, all this would change with the construction of south and north walls. The harbour began to silt up. By 1836, a reference to Clontarf harbour describes it as enclosed. Local trade, fishing and philanthropy were seen as subservient to the demands of the city. The harbour would never recover.

A Consummate Bibliophile – Notes

In 1593, Dublin corporation compelled two Dublin merchants to remove 'the carcas of the oud Hulke ... from which great daunger growth to ships coming into the Pole of Clontarfe (Brady, K., 2008). The merchants, under threat of prison, were John Forster and Skypper Berns (De Courcy, 1996).

The Knights Templars grew wheat and barley for beer (it seems); they also levied taxes on mills in the area (Lennon, 2012).

On absentee landlords (D'Alton, John, 1838, *The History of the County of Dublin*, Dublin, Hodges and Smith).

On a pirate encounter (Lennon, 2012).

On anchorage tax (McIntyre, 1987). Salt was being imported into Clontarf Pool for use at Contarf in 1630 (De Courcy, 1996).

On 1641 (Curry, J., 1793, *An Historical and Critical Review of the Civil Wars in Ireland*, Dublin, P. Wogan). Luke Netterville had earlier seized and plundered a vessel with his supporters.

Christmas Weekes Esq was an occasional attender at general meetings of the Royal Dublin Society (1816-25). Weeks appeared to have spent much of his time in his library, replete with 'the most valuable works in the republic of letters'.

On Weekes (Bowden, C.T., 1791, *A Tour Through Ireland*, Dublin, W. Corbet).

The Down Survey map of 1658 appears to map the Sheds area as 'Harogs town' (Scandanavian?). A map of 1728 by Charles Brooking in the *Healy Collection* marks an area near here as 'The Herring Shelds', and slightly further on 'The Brick Kilns'.

By 1806, fish were no longer cured at the Sheds (Sleater, Matthew, 1806, *Introductory Essay to a New System of Civil and Ecclesiastical Topography*, Bolton Street, Barlow).

Archaeological digs at 76 Clontarf Park indicate that springs are present in the Sheds area (www.excavations.ie). Knowles states that an old jetty at Vernon Avenue was covered up by the promenade. Also under the promenade are two dead horses, household refuse and a boat known as 'riddles boat' (Knowles, 1970).

Around 1719, a ship's crew could probably also have taken advantage of a building known as the Sign of the Ship, presumably an inn, which in 1764 may have become known as the Sign of the Star and Garter. It is speculated that a 1785 sketch by Francis Wheatley may have included a building known as the fish house or a Revenue building (Gogarty, 2013).

'The furlong' appears to have stretched as far as the oyster beds – about 200 metres. De Courcy (1996) observes that it was mentioned by Sir John Terrell in 1603 in the riding of the franchises and that it may have extended in an indefinite manner towards Clontarf Baths and Island.

Harbours on the south of the Liffey, particularly Ringsend, were equally if not more important.

On the platform (De Courcy, 1996).

Weekes' wharf may also be the wharf visible in J. La Porte's etching of the Clontarf Sheds in 1796 (De Courcy, 1996).

On the enclosed harbour (Jeffrey, 1977).

The harbour's decline was further exacerbated by Clontarf failing to build up a large suburban population in the nineteenth century. It lay close to the disreputable and dangerous Ballybough and also the Fairview sloblands; the Vernons restrictively controlled much of the land and acquired a veto over any Clontarf township improvements; the railway had not been built; there was periodic flooding; tolls also existed to the north of the city and potential sewage construction brought the fear of contagion (Daly, M., 2011, *Dublin: The Deposed Capital – A Social and Economic History, 1860-1914*, Cork, Cork University Press).

14

The Nightingale and the Mermaid

In 1822, the poet William Hamilton Drummond conjured up the area in his verse 'Clontarf, a poem'. Drummond describes Crab Lake as a small channel across which children could wade at low water. The lake possessed cockles, razor and shellfish. Drummond also notes the presence of salicornia (which he recognised could be used for glassmaking) and eryngo – sea holly. The eryngo had edible roots, and because of its beauty Drummond would call it the queen of the vegetable race. Drummond also appears to have found a sea mouse. Its scientific name – *Aphrodita aculeate* – derives from Aphrodite, the goddess of love, supposedly on account of the fact that when viewed ventrally it resembles female genitalia. It is unlikely that Drummond would have agreed: the hair on his sea mouse was of beautiful green and orange colours mixed with black prickles. Before the poem descends into a homage to nationalism and Henry Grattan – by way of its Viking-inspired bloodfest – it also speaks of euphorbia (a purgative) and the mew (gull), curlew (which sings its own name), plover and the sandlark, the 'nightingale of the ocean'.

Drummond was conscious that there was tragedy aplenty on the North Bull. Seemingly riding high on local lore and the imagination of a classical education, he poetically ascribed the Bull's many shipwrecks to mermaids. A local Dublin story recounted 12 years later in the *Dublin Penny Journal* puts it the other way around. Supposedly, sometime in the eighteenth century, two ships from New York were wrecked on the North Bull, and two so-called 'mermaids' named Mary and Rachel Pigeon had rowed across from the nearby Pigeon House in dark stormy waters to the rescue. They found two men on a plank; one paddling astride, the other on his back lying exhausted. On his breast he clutched a child, snapped at by waves. In a film today, all this would have ended in marriage – for both women. And in the possibly confabulating *Dublin Penny Journal* it did as well. It's not certain if the story had any substance, and it is clear that the text would rather mythologise the women than recognise their efforts. Earlier, on 31 December 1807, the *Augusta Connor* had indeed been lost on the North Bull. Only the Captain, mate and two boys were saved. But Rachel and Mary's rescue seems to have occurred in 1767 – and saved only one boy and a man.

Drummond notes that one particular shipwreck had been discovered on the Bull near Clontarf by locals actively digging in a time of scarcity around 1761. These locals were almost certainly not casually fuel or treasure hunting on the Bull. For centuries catastrophic deforestation right across Ireland meant fuel was no longer abundantly available from the countryside. The few woods still visible at Clontarf in Greenville's 1686 map are replaced by arable land in Rocque's more detailed map of 1756. Indeed, land around Clontarf had long been used for tillage and grazing. Much of it that was likely to contain trees was probably under the control of private estates. Anything that had been left in the immediate vicinity may have been further decimated as a result of the 'Great Frost' of 1741. When the temperature plummeted in this unprecedented European climatic shock the Liffey froze over. Scallops and prawns died in the water. Snipe, small birds and field hares died. People perished. Fortunately for the digging locals, fuel was duly salvaged – as were a silver plate, stand and six bottles of fine wine found in the hold (the news was sufficiently exciting to make William Maitland's *London Chronicle*).

The Nightingale and the Mermaid – Notes

Drummond, W. H., 1822, *Clontarf, a Poem*, Dublin, Archer.

Drummond's Sea Holly: 'With clustering florets, whose light antlers dance in the fresh breeze like tiny topaz gems.'

A passing reference to vampires in Drummond also makes you wonder if Bram Stoker, who frequently walked the area, was familiar with the work – though the literature of the period is admittedly replete with them.

Plover was good food, equal to duck, according to Rutty (1771).

Drummond on Mermaids: 'Oft we heard the tale of mermaids rising from their coral grots, / And as they combed their oozy tresses green / Chanting such strains of witching harmony, / as in oblivion wrapt the sailor's soul...'

On the rescue (Hardy, P. D., 1834, *The Dublin Penny Journal*, pp. 99-101).

On the *Augusta Connor* (Anon., 1808, January 10, *The National Register*, p. 30).

On Rachel and Mary's rescue (Brady, K., 2008).

Local lore recalled that an unnamed ship had been wrecked on the Bull 18 years prior to 1761.

By the fifteenth and sixteenth centuries many regions (though by no means all) were treeless or possessed only scattered tree cover. Reasons included the charcoal industry, shipbuilding, clearing for crops, cask making, tanning, fuel harvesting, insecurity of tenancy, the perception that they sheltered rebels and bandits etc. (Kenneth Nichols in Duffy, P.J., Edwards, D. and Fitzpatrick, E., 2004, *Gaelic Ireland,* Dublin, Four Courts Press).

Keating's 1634 *Foras Feasa ar Éirinn* claims Nín, son of Béil, found all of Ireland (*Inis na bh-Fiodhbhadh* – Island of the woods) to be forest with the exception of *Magh-n-ealta* alone. Keating's origin myth also claims Partholanus died there ('f*uair Partholón bás ar Sheanmháigh Ealta Eadair*') and that flocks of Irish birds came to bask there in the sun ('*tigdís eunlaith Éireann d'á ngrianghoradh*').

The Snipe: 'sniping up with plaintive cry' in Uinsin O'Donovan's poem 'Bull Island' (McIntyre, 1987).

The Liffey also froze over in 1338 and 1845 (De Courcy, 1996).

On finding wine (Maitland, W.F., 1761, *The London Chronicle*, Vol IX).

15

The Meadow of the Bull

By the time Drummond authored his poem, the bank was known to be increasing in height and cattle were grazing in summer. And certainly after the wall was built, what was perhaps once ephemeral and transient quickly became something more stable. In 1844, sheep would summer on marine grasses. And by 1865, it was suggested that the island could even be used to quarantine imported cattle and the diseases they carried.

The more ancient etymology of the word Clontarf, in Irish *Cluain Tairbh*, is believed to signify 'The meadow of the bull', which conjures up yet more grazing cattle with ancient pre-Christian and medieval minders. And so the much more recent naming of Bull Island, in Irish *Oileán an Tairbh*, would appear quite fitting. However, although the South Bull strand *did* have an area known at 'The Green Patch' – at least as far back as 1728 – nothing similar appears to have been the case for the North Bull sands. Indeed, Drummond, whose poem was written before the North Bull Wall was constructed, had been told that within living memory *not a blade of grass* had ever grown on the bank. That said, coastal sea levels around Ireland have altered dramatically over the millennia. So it's always possible that the modern etymology has accidentally been superimposed on some historical truth – but we don't have any evidence for such a claim. The earliest map of the city, John Speed's 1610 map, simply illustrates *sand* north of the river. The sands are labelled 'Clantarf'.

Drummond consequently argued that the Bull sand bank, after which the island takes its name, was so called on account of the loud, bellowing waves. Although it's also possible that Bull derives from Ball, meaning an offshore sand bank. In one way or another, however, the name can be associated with sand banks – and so we find the use of 'bull' in other Irish coastal place names.

The Meadow of the Bull – Notes

On sheep (Fraser, 1844). Grass or no grass, French texts still referred Bull Island as '*une île de sable*' as late as 1928.

On quarantine (Anon., 1865, August 16, 'The Cattle Detained', *The Irish Times*, p. 2); a fear of cattle plague was noted in the *Dublin Daily Express* in 1866 (Daly, 2011).

Wilde (1857) speaks of the enclosure of the two Bulls: *Cluan dá tarbh*.

On the ancient and modern races of oxen in Ireland (*Proceedings of the Royal Irish Academy*, vol. 7, pp. 64-75).

The North Bay coast has long been inhabited: Bronze age axe heads have been found in Clontarf. The hill of Howth, once an island, possesses, among other things, one megalithic portal tomb, one cairn (Dun Hill), and a kerbed cairn (Shelmartin). 'Kitchen middens' were also found at Sutton Cross, indicating the presence of Neolithic humans around 3000 BC (De Courcy, 1996). Tumuli were also once present near Clontarf Station (Westropp, T.J., 1904).

Dollymount strand possibly owes its etymology to Dorothy or Dolly Vernon, but this is not at all certain. Dawson rejects the naming association with the daughter of Sir George Haddon and states the name first appears on a house in the area (Dawson, T., 1976, 'The road to Howth', *Dublin Historical Record*, 29(4), pp. 122-132). This seems to be correct. John Brownrig's 1792 map shows an area called Dollymount in possession of a military officer (NLI. MS 21 F. 51 / (079)).

The Irish name *Baile na gcorr* is also associated with the area in 1923 and possibly from as early as 1777. This could mean town of the cranes, sand eels or other birds. See detailed etymological arguments re cranes and the word *corr* (Bhaldraithe, P., 2012, 'True of false? The Crane Revisited', *Archaeology Ireland*, 26(2), 22-24). It has also been speculated that Kincora translates to *Ceann Cora*, the head of the crane. Some locals speculate that this name may have derived from the former morphology of nearby costal features. North Bull Island is translated into Irish as *An Bulla Thuaidh*.

On the green patch, see the 1728 Charles Brooking map in the Healy Collection (www.southdublinlibraries.ie).

In 1837, Samuel Lewis described the North Bull as a long strip of sandy ground, partly green, surrounded on all sides by water. By 1838, the Bull is described as possessing a sickly verdure (D'Alton, 1838).

In the past, the coastline was different and extended inland. In 1908, Clontarf mains drainage along St Anne's Park (hence probably James Larkin road) burrowed through sand to a depth of 28 feet (Anon., 1908, October 3, *Freeman's Journal*, p. 4).

On Bull deriving from Ball, meaning an offshore sand bank (McIntyre, 1987). Flood considered the idea of a roaring surf supplying the name's origin as fanciful (Flood, D.T., 1975, *Dublin Historical Record*, Vol. 28, No. 4, pp. 142-153).

16

Lady Kane

As we have seen, the Sewage and Land Reclamation Company sought to characterise the Bull merely as waste land (a term much loved by developers). But there is no evidence to suggest that this was the case. In 1833, Lady Katherine Bailey Kane noted that Ireland was largely uncharted territory for the botanist. The information did exist, but Ireland was a 'closed book' because all the native plants – well documented by Irish herbalists – were written in Gaelic.

This was not exactly true. It was only a matter of making inquiries: Trelkeld, for example, did interchangeably supply Irish, Latin and English names. Nevertheless, rather than bother to interact with the Irish plant names, Lady Katherine proceeded to remap and colonise Irish flora with the scientific nomenclature of Carl Linnaeus and a post-enlightenment zeal for accuracy. This was fortunate. In doing so, she remapped the environs of Clontarf and the many plants which would ultimately characterise Bull Island as an area of outstanding natural beauty, and an area worthy of conservation and the later appellation biosphere.

Among a dazzle of Latin and botanical trainspotting we find hare's foot trefoil noted along 'the sandbanks' from Clontarf to Sutton. At the salt marshes in Clontarf she notes salt-marsh club-rush, sea milk-wort and sea arrow grass. Along the sandy seashore at Clontarf: dwarf sea wheat grass. At the marshy shores from Clontarf to Sutton: sea goosefoot. Along the gravelly shore from Clontarf to Sutton: sea catchfly. On the seashore between Clontarf and Sutton: corn sow-thistle and sea feverfew. On the banks along the seashore between Clontarf and Raheny: lesser meadow-rue. At the banks between Clontarf and Sutton: wild thyme. At Clontarf: sea rocket and sea starwort. On the commons along the shore below Clontarf: common mallow.

Lady Katherine further records along the shore from Clontarf to Howth, lambs lettuce, sea plantain, round-fruited rush, sea sandwort, common scurvy grass and jagged-leaved crane's bill. Along the seashore leading to Clontarf: creeping sea sweet grass. Along the steep banks between Clontarf and Kilbarrack: Great Fescue-grass (nearly four feet high), wild teasel (four feet high), common gromwell. And along the shore from Clontarf to Kilbarrack: common reed (six feet high).

The magnificence of Lady Katherine's undertaking is worth comparing to one of her peers. Three years later, in 1836, James Makay, associate of the Linnaean Society and member of the Royal Irish Academy, makes only a few slight references to the flora of Clontarf. He found hairy violet, field chickweed and glacuous clubrush to be plentiful along the sea between Clontarf and Kilbarrack. He did not reference the North Bull itself. However, by the 1830s the North Bull was most definitely heaving with life.

In 1838, writer and naturalist John D'Alton made specific observations about the North Bull. He recorded dwarf sea grass, catchfly, wild teasel (whose seeds the European gold-finch likes) and jagged leaved crane's bill. Speaking of the salt marshes, D'Alton further recorded salt marsh club rush, sea milk (black saltwort), sea goose foot, sea arrow grass, and red and white campion (bachelor's button). An entire cornuco-pia of life was present: sea plantain, common groundsel, wild spinach (sea beet), prickly saltwort, coriander, sea sandwort, yellow horned poppy, lesser meadow rue, common scurvy grass, Danish scurvy-grass, sea rocket, common mallow, sea starwort, sea feverfew, little bulbous rush, great sharp rush, round fruited rush field chickweed and glaucous club rush.

Later enthusiasts would add to this collection. Old man's beard (or travellers' joy) and shore bindweed, for example, were noted in 1892. Yet by the turn of the century, the grow-ing pressures of human recreation on the Bull means a shift in emphasis among botanists becomes noticeable. By 1909, President George H. Pathybridge (PhD BSc) of the Dublin Naturalists Field Club can be found lecturing on the North Bull and its problems.

Lady Kane – Notes

Lady Katherine notes respectively: f.olitoria, p.maritima, j.compressus, a.peploides, c.officinalis, g.dissectum, s. maritimus, g.maritima, t.maritimum, g.maritima, f.elatior, d.sylvestris, l.officinale, a.phragmites, t.loliaceum, ch.maritimum, s.maritima, s.arvensis, p.maritimum, t.serpyllum, c.maritima, a.tripolium, var. sylvestris var. m underwoodiana, and t.arvense.

MacKay, J. T., 1836, *Flora Hibernica*, Dublin, William Curry.

MacKay notes respectively: v.hirta, c.arvense and s.glaucous; in 1824, MacKay, in an attempt to chart all of Ireland's plants (374 genera and 935 species), reported very little concerning the Bull (though he charts much at Howth). He notes: Scirpus in a salt marsh between Clontarf and Kilbarrick Church; Bromus in the sandy meadows between Clontarf and Howth; Euphorbia on the strand between Clontarf and Howth; cerastium near Sutton and at Kilbarrick; and papaver, myosotis, tifolium, lycopsis, vicia and senecio on the sandy fields near Kilbarrack Church. Mackay seems to have stopped at Kilbarrack and Howth but for reasons unclear seems to have passed over Clontarf (Mackay, J.T., 1825, 'Catalogue of the Indigenous Plants of Ireland', *The Transactions of the Royal Irish Academy*, vol 14, pp. 103-198).

From the Sheds to Blackbush – near what is now the nearby St Anne's park and before Watermill road and bridge – D'Alton (1838) also found 'wild clary' (wild sage) and the somewhat nutty flavoured lambs lettuce. The hairy violet (*Viola hirta*) was later reported on the coast from Clontarf to Kilbarrick [sic] (Anon., 1854, 'Flowers for March', *The Catholic Layman*, 3(27), p. 41).

In 1892, McArdle lists *Clematis vitabla, Convolvulus soldanella, Leymus arenarius, Triticum junceum* (McArdle, D., 1892, 'Clematis vitabla, L., on the North Bull, Dollymount, Co. Dublin', *The Irish Naturalist*, 1(6), p. 125).

On problems (Anon., 1909, January 18, 'Dublin Naturalist Field Club', *The Irish Times*).

17

The Sand Witches

The island emerged from the sea in the 1820s just as Irish conchology – the study of shells and their inhabitants – was reaching its high water mark. In this curious proto-Victorian world, authors such as Dr. William Turton (translator of Linnaeus and author of the 1816 catalogue *Irish Conchology*) had gained a particular foothold in the annals of international conchology.

Turton's *Conchological Dictonary* of 1819 is replete with 'testacea' (invertebrate animals covered with shells) of mind-bogglingly complex descriptions. To the excitement of collectors, new species such as *Venus antiqua* and *Mytilus velutinus,* and the rare *Venus tigeriana,* were all found in Dublin Bay. Ditto for the presence of *Turbo Cingillus, Chiton cinereus,* and the *Turbo pentanglularis* found by Turton himself. In the same location, the much sought for *Venus undata* was also 'taken alive'. This was a happier event for the collector than it was for the creatures that inhabited the shells. They could be extracted with hot water.

One particular force in this scientific endeavour, however, was formally excluded from higher education, but had always been socially linked with shells: women. In 1819, Turton would acknowledge the calibre of a Ms. Lawless – who in one excursion alone had collected 100 species at Portmarnock – as 'a naturalist of rare and excellent distinction'. Lawless was seemingly not an exception. One writer could later observe of the Bull that, 'a friend of mine tells me that the number of young ladies who read and pick up shells there, and whom he calls sand witches, is decidedly on the increase'.

The prospect of finding a scientific novelty was a very real possibility. As such, across Dublin, shells were being eagerly catalogued and polished by many avid collectors, amateur and professional, including Lawless herself. These often exchanged hands for a high price – with alert fishmongers and fishermen often getting a cut. The shells finally came to rest in places such as the museum at Trinity or Dublin's scattered curiosity cabinets, including a *Tellina jugosa* quickly transferred to the cabinet of one Dr. Taylor, having been found in the blue clay off Clontarf.

Some scientific interest in bivalves continued in the next century, albeit at a lesser pace. In 1943, for example, the Natural History Museum acquired pearls from Clontarf's blue mussels (*Mytilus edulis*). Today a small black box, with a glass lid and navy velvet display background, reveals this scattering of small pearls, as fine as sand – the biggest no more than 4 millimetres (in the display, the mussel appears as a bountiful resource – but in fact the pearls are rare).

Specific historic evidence for finds at Clontarf and the Bull sands is surprisingly sketchy, though they certainly abounded in mussel, oysters, razor fish and cockles. Samples from Dollymount were donated by one Ms Wright in 1899 (including items such as *Macta stultorum, Chamelea gallina, Vererupis senegalensis*). Numerous shells of the genera *Solen, Tellina, Mactra, Venus, Tapes, Pectum* and *Cardium* were also found on the island by the Dublin Naturalist Field Club in 1917, with several more collected and described by a Miss Colgan in 1919. But many collectors often simply located finds to 'Dublin Bay'. The display cabinets of the island's interpretive centre now hold shells such as the common whelk, turret shells, Icelandic mussel, pelican's foot, sand gaper, spiny cockle and sea urchins – aka the spiny hedgehog or Aristotle's lantern.

The Sand Witches – Notes

Turton was assisted by his daughter, whose name he hides from us, but possibly reveals in a double urn image showing two faces.

Another notable author was Thomas Brown (with accounts such as *Irish Testacea*).

Turton had a bivalve – the turtonia – named after him.

In 1835, Robert Grant in *The Dublin Journal of Medical Science* would ridicule descriptive conchology as an 'injudicious' mode of study, opting instead for the supposedly more profitable science of comparative anatomy. The science persisted nonetheless.

On sand witches (Anon., 1873, August 23, *The Nation*, p. 10).

John Nutall and M.J. O'Kelly were other notable collectors.

On blue clay (Wartburton, J., Whitelaw, J. and Walsh, R., 1818).

The cockles make it into 'Song of the Dublin Jarvey': 'If you want to drive round Dublin / Sure you'll find me on the stand / I'll take you to Raheny for cockles on the strand' (Crosbie, P., 1981, *Your Dinner's Poured Out!* Dublin, O'Brien Press).

On mussels (D'Alton, 1838).

The isthmus of Howth and Portmarnock were also dense with shells.

Wright's donation (National Museum Northern Ireland: NMINH 1899.66 http://www.habitas.org.uk).

On the field club trip (Anon., 1917, 'Irish societies', *The Irish Naturalist*, 26(10), pp. 166-168).

Colgan's collection (National Museum Northern Ireland: NMINH 1919.102 http://www.habitas.org.uk).

18

Kid Gloves

Nature doesn't do innocence – it eats it. In 1953, one of the island's most celebrated ornithologists, P.G. Kennedy, reported a peregrine swooping on a flock of starlings and carrying one off to the consternation of the rest. Ravens had also been spotted by Kennedy feasting on Dunlin in the sand bunkers. Yet other birds had been found dead on the fairway – seemingly having been mobbed by lapwings. In terms of basic diet, an oystercatcher is capable of devouring over 200 cockles in a day, other birds much more. And the Bull sands make for magnificent feeding grounds. Small wonder then that in 1977, palaeontologist D.C. Palmer's overview of the shelly invertebrates would morbidly admit that to the casual observer there was more evidence of *death* than life on the beach.

Many of the shells strewn on the beach then were once the sartorial extravagances of a variety of violently disposed of creatures. However, the best example of nature's violence on the Bull may not be that of a shell.

In 1857, an unusual parcel was found on the Bull sands. Inside the parcel was a dress shirt – finely plaited. Also inside were six inches of sleeves, a pair of wrist bands and the ends of the body of a shirt. These portions were cut from the garment to which they belonged, and not torn off. They constituted portions of clothing of some 'respectable' person – seemingly a man.

A white Indian silk neckerchief was also found in the parcel, with a piece cut out of its centre. The inserted shirt front bore several marks of blood or something strongly resembling it. The stud holes were torn as if the studs had been violently pulled out. Around the hole were dark red stains. Unsurprisingly, the *Freeman's Journal* suspected the respectable person had met with foul play – and that the other fragments of his clothing had been destroyed or concealed elsewhere. But no corpse was ever reported. The *Freeman's Journal* could only write it up as a 'mysterious occurrence'.

Such an event naturally casts conspiratorial – yet unsupportable – suspicions on the immediate period that follows. Four years later, in 1861, a woman went out for a walk on the Bull Wall one July evening and disappeared. She was presumed to have fallen off the wall and drowned. A rattled *Freeman's Journal* described it as a 'mysterious disappearance'. Two years later, in 1863, the body of an unknown female with laced boots was found on the strand, but this got little attention. In 1865, a boat was discovered on the North Bull – lying bottom up. This time the *Freeman's Journal* described it as a 'strange case'. Under the boat, a coat was discovered. In the pocket an Indian rubber tobacco pouch, kid gloves and a new briar tobacco pouch. The man who earlier hired it from Ringsend was nowhere to be seen. He was feared drowned.

Conspiracy also lent itself to events in 1915, which forced the *Irish Independent* to declare that all suspicions of a murder tragedy had been dispelled: The body of a 35-year-old woman had washed ashore near the North Bull. She was wearing a brown skirt. Her coat had an underskirt of blue serge. There were kid gloves on her hands. Covered by the left hand glove was a sum of two shillings and sixpence. A brooch bore the words, 'A present from South End'. The remains were not – as had been stated in some quarters – enclosed in a sack. In 1925, P. Duffy's black overcoat, shoes and socks were found at the end of the Bull Wall – but seemingly not P. Duffy.

Like the winter winds on the island, the destructive and self-destructive tendencies of human nature can chill to the bone. It is that part of nature that throws nature against itself. It is ever present and cannot be avoided. On the telephone wires near the clubhouse, I spot a murder of crows.

Kid Gloves – Notes

On ravens in bunkers (Kennedy, 1935).

On Palmer's observations (Jeffrey, 1977).

On dress shirt found (Anon., 1857, November 17, 'Mysterious Occurrence', *Freeman's Journal*, p. 3).

On woman who disappeared (Anon., 1861, July 13, *Freeman's Journal*, p. 3; Reynolds, M., 1869, August 29, 'I buried my love alive there', *Freeman's Journal*, p. 2).

On woman with laced boots (Anon., 1863, August 17, *Freeman's Journal*, p. 3).

On kid gloves (Anon., 1865, July 5, 'A Strange Case', *Freeman's Journal*, p. 3). A boating tragedy in the same year, which resulted in the deaths of five gentlemen, did not seem odd to the paper (Anon., 1865, August 12, 'The five missing gentlemen', *The Nation*, p. 18). Nor the supposed boating tragedy of a member of the ballast board and another man in 1867 (Anon., 1867, July 6, 'How to shoot', *The Nation*, p. 9).

The reasons for suspicions in the case of the 35-year-old woman are unclear (Anon., 1915, January 4, *Irish Independent*, p. 6).

On P. Duffy (Anon., 1925, August 15, 'Miss Rita', *Southern Star*, p. 3).

19

The War on Birds

Immediately prior to the appearance of the island, the birds of Dublin were charted by John Rutty in 1771. This was as much an act of menu planning as ornithological cataloguing. Pride of anecdotal place went to the Isle of Man puffin, which was killed, salted and barrelled, then imported to Dublin to be eaten with potatoes. But nearly anything with wings was considered 'fair game'. As with the finds from earlier Viking excavations, birds that we might see on the Bull today, such as curlew, gulls, redshank and 'most delicious' teal, were all on the menu. The mackerel cock (Manx shearwater) was not spared. Nor the dirty 'shag', although on occasion a bird such as the greater sea swallow might escape, being 'intolerably filthy' and 'rank'.

It is tempting to confirm the presence of large numbers of birds near the Bull sands in the eighteenth century, but evidence from Rutty is only suggestive. In fact, in Rutty's account only the redshank, teal, and bulls eye (sea lark) are actually described as being from 'the strand' (the latter eating sea fleas and also found in marsh), which could of course be a lot of places in Dublin. Hence it is impossible to know from Rutty if various named birds such as the 'sea parrot' (Atlantic puffin) or sea eagle (sea osprey), which Rutty did locate to Lambay Island, spent any time on the North Bull's low tidal sands prior to the island's emergence. Guessing is made all the more treacherous by the fact that, as with the puffin, many birds were imported for eating, and that Rutty has borrowed from other sources. Rutty does note vagrants and other winter and summer migrants, but again not their nesting place.

All we know for certain is that Rutty found cockles on the Bull, and that birds fed on them. Similarly, in 1686, Greenville appears to have marked 'Herronstown' at Clontarf next to the North Bull. This perhaps suggests the presence of its name sake – but perhaps more likely an individual's surname (a Captain Heron is connected with Howth around 1566) or even a name stemming from local herring fishing. Nevertheless, in the years prior to the construction of the wall, the importance of the Bull feeding grounds and coastal habitats to Irish birds must have been steadily growing. As we have seen, Irish forestry had been decimated in the previous 300 years, and by 1800 cover stood at less than 1 per cent. Many local bird habitats had been utterly obliterated. And inland traditions of bird trapping, hunting and so forth were increasingly unsustainable (though by no means wiped out). The growing sands at the North Bull – now available even at high tide – would have been an increasingly rich and important source of local nourishment for any bird populations already present – and doubtless for displaced flocks.

Perhaps on account of habitat destruction elsewhere, and regardless of their numbers, the birds in the area now appear to become increasingly visible. In 1809, for example, a Miss Battersby (possibly Mary) paints two separate watercolours of birds from the Clontarf area: a golden plover and a sand lark. In 1825, Brewer mused that some Irish writers suggested that Howth took its name from *Ben Hadar*, 'the bird's promontory', on account of the fact that 'the rocks on this coast are still the resort of unusual numbers of sea foul'. Irrespective of its etymological accuracy, the statement thus confirms that unusal numbers of sea birds were resident near the Bull in 1825. And by 1838, John D'Alton could note that clouds of starlings, in numbers *exceeding belief*, would descend on the North Bull 'like locusts of the east' and pass the nights in the reeds.

It was not the only thing in the reeds: 'carnage' ensued when the somewhat less visible boatmen 'slaughtered' them in their hundreds with their guns. Strictly speaking, killing birds was not something you could do willy-nilly at this time. Since 1828, a number of *Game Acts* and a *Night Poaching Act* existed across Ireland. These provided a modicum of protection to the kinds of birdlife that would later be recorded on the island: widgeon, plover, wild ducks, snipe and teal. Nevertheless, at this time such laws seem to have had limited value on and around the Bull.

Ornithologists themselves were particularly keen hunters. In 1845, for example, when J. J. Watters – author of the *Natural History of the Birds of Ireland* – saw a flock of five gadwall flying past the wooden bridge, he promptly shot an adult male. Similarly, William Thompson, author of *The Natural History of Ireland,* would shoot a glaucous gull in 1849. For such agents the prize remained great. In addition to the scientific prestige of acquiring new knowledge, social praise could also be obtained for contributing to museum collections, or bagging a 'bird of the year'. Personal satisfaction continued to be obtained through possessing an extensive private collection.

(This did not of course guarantee preservation: the collection of Watters perished by fire; museums would also struggle with pest control.)

In 1869, some of the island's birds gained more extensive protection from an act of parliament: *The Sea Birds Preservation Act*. The act gave legal sanctuary during the breeding season and covered 'the different species of auk, bonxie, Cornish chough, coulterneb, diver, eider duck, fulmar, gannet, grebe, guillemot, gull, kittiwake, loon, marrot, merganser, murre, oyster catcher, petrel, puffin, razor bill, scout, seamew, sea parrot, sea swallow, shearwater, shelldrake, skua, smew, solan goose, tarrock, tern, tystey, willock'. Such legislation was not necessarily motivated by kindness. Birds were desired for food and objects of sport (some birds were needed for hawking). They were also useful for controlling rooks that preyed on farmer's crops and were seen as a useful asset in alerting fishermen to the presence of fish or rocks.

For all that, things continued much as before – with a special eye being kept for less common varieties. In 1884, for example, J.J. Dowling would note the shooting by 'fowlers' of duck and snipe but also woodcock – a casual visitor on migration. Dowling also wrote the following in the same year:

> The tide was falling when I reached the bridge, and soon a flock of gulls passed over me. I noticed one of them, which seemed different from any bird I had previously met, and having missed him with the first barrel I brought him down with the second – winged.

Dowling then presented the dead bird to the National Museum, Dublin.

Public, private and scientific interest in the birds of the Bull was growing. This interest is reflected in the current contents of the Natural History Museum, established by the Royal Dublin Society in 1857. This so-called dead zoo (now a museum of a museum) retains much of its nineteenth century character. And today its antiquated glass cabinets still nest many birds from the Bull. They bear dusty witness to the morbid curiosity of the late nineteenth and early twentieth century: a great black backed gull (from 1877), a stone curlew (1885), a spotted redshank (1890), a male guillemot (1898), a sanderling (1899), two male grey plover in summer and winter plumage (1899 and 1900), and a female bar tailed godwit in winter plumage (1901). A common shelduck in its first year's plumage (apparently purchased in 1902) is also present in this mausoleum. Photography would soon surpass this mode of communication. In 1899, Charles Patten, for example, could photograph the depression of a little tern on the Dollymount shingle and thereby explain in detail the construction of the tern's nest.

Nineteenth century interest in Irish birds culminated in the publication of Ussher and Warren's comprehensive *Birds of Ireland* of *1900*. Among other things, this comprehensive work charted the presence of a snowy owl in the winter of 1880-1881 (a rare and uncertain visitor) and the 'rare and accidental' presence of an avocet in 1897. The book further noted that the only specimen of the 'extremely rare' Kentish plover known to exist in Ireland was a male that came from the Bull (then in the Montgomery collection at the Science and Art Museum, Dublin). Knot and large numbers of sanderling were also charted. Redpoll fed on the 'wart wort' and other plants, whose seeds were also eaten by snow bunting. And the bar tailed godwit was also common – except in severe winters.

The various observations came via correspondence from interested agents such as Edward Williams, Blake Knox and Dr. Charles J. Patten, and from writing in various sources such as More's *List of Irish Birds*. This led to a new problem for ornithologists: as the quantity of material increased (along with the number of investigators) fewer and less striking new 'discoveries' were possible. Hence in 1900 Richard Barrington's fascinating study *The Migration of Birds as Observed at Irish Lighthouses* (recorded from 1881 onwards) would complain that, 'it becomes more difficult year by year to discover anything new, especially about our common English birds'. The fact that the 'low fruit' on the scientific tree had been picked would in part contribute to a growing shift in the interests of ornithologists towards bird conservation, via legislation, activism and the creation of bird sanctuaries.

Bird hazards, for example, were now being charted. More's *List of Irish Birds* had already noted that owing to poisoning the sea eagle had become rarer than the golden eagle. And from 1880-1894, legislation further evolved in a series of *Wild Birds Protection Acts*, so that the number of protected birds in Ireland rose to 86, including the oystercatcher, godwit, dunlin, shoveler and short eared owl – otherwise known in Ireland as the fern owl – all of which can still be spotted on the island today. But for reasons unclear, an 1896 act that counted over 335 birds did not apply to Ireland.

As with before, it is difficult to believe that these laws were effective or held any persuasive power on or around the Bull. The first apparent prosecution relating to birds in the area only occurred in 1889, and this only concerned licences and stock control – not the act of shooting birds itself (brothers John and George Reynolds were prosecuted at Coolock Petty Sessions for shooting two plover – they had failed to produce licences to a witness employed by the Society for the Preservation of Game). Shooting rarities was still socially acceptable. In 1903, a reader quite nonchalantly writes to the *Freeman's Journal* to tell of his experience bagging a then 'very rare ornithological specimen', which he labelled a 'Dutch marine cormorant'. In 1906, a glossy ibis – rare on the island – was also happily shot.

Even when caught, criminals appeared to have remained undeterred by low punitive sanctions. In 1906, Michael Divine – a bird fancier – was found trying to 'nab birds' on the island. Divine had used a net and put out decoy birds in his attempt to catch wild birds, and a nest had been found with four young skylarks, all dead – the hen had been caught. And the bird dealer, who had initially given a false name, was given the choice of becoming a jailbird himself or paying a small fine. This appears to have been the same undeterred 'bird catcher' Devine, who caught a Richard's pippet near Kilbarrack Church while netting larks at night around October 1911 (now on display in the Natural History Museum).

Nevertheless, the laws did in fact have some seasonal effects. By 1908, the 'crying evil' of constant Sunday shooting on the North Bull had stopped, and poulterers' shops whose wares of dead white fronted geese and golden plover 'often grieved humane bird lovers' could no longer stock out of season. The laws also lent defenders of the birds a degree of moral authority, which they could attempt to use to their advantage. In 1910, the Dublin Society for the Prevention of Cruelty to Animals (est. 1840) highlighted the cruelty of shooting birds at the North Bull – where shot birds were left to die in the water. Such crimes, they needed to remind the public, were prosecutable. Special instructions were given to inspectors to watch out for offenders. Leading members of the ISPB also continued to advocate for a 'cessation of the war on birds' and against their 'wanton slaughter'.

The War on Birds – Notes

Crow feathers were used for writing and harpsichords; swan feathers for artists pencils and ornamental hats; geese feathers for beds. Birds could be reared, snared, hawked or shot (as Rutty did to a pop jack in 1755). The yellow water wagtail was recommended for houses to catch flies, owls for mice. How to nurse a number of other birds is also mentioned – perhaps to nurse them back to full health before eating them. Or to harvest eggs. It seems some were probably kept by Rutty for their song. Rutty himself had birds caged for over a year but notes the hedge sparrow, though a good singer, was not suitable for a cage. Nursing also improved their song (oddly enough).

The name 'bulls eye' was suggested to have originated from the size of its eye. It had nothing to do with the Bull sands.

Puffins have certainly been present within the boundary of the Bull sanctuary (Kennedy, P.G., 1953, *An Irish Sanctuary: Birds of the North Bull*, Dublin, The Sign of the Three Candles).

On herons (Hore, H. F., 1853, 'The hosting against the Northern Irish in 1566', *Ulster Journal of Archaeology*, 1, pp. 159-163).

On unusual numbers of sea foul (Brewer, J.N., 1825, *The Beauties of Ireland*, London, Sherwood Jones and Co.).

The common reed was noted on the shore of the North Bull; a number of marshy areas existed along the coastline and at Howth. At Howth, cliffs provided good bird habitats.

In 1847, two men could also be found shooting on the island (where one seriously wounded his companion) (Anon., 1847, August 2, *Freeman's Journal*, p. 4).

On five gadwell (Kennedy, 1953).

Thompson noted three dead stint on the Bull in 1831; 60 little stint are noted present in 1892 in Ussher and Warren (1900).

On Thompson shooting a glaucous gull (Kennedy, 1953).

On Watters collection (Ussher and Warren, 1900).

The breeding season was defined as April first to August first. The Lord Lieutenant of Ireland was permitted to extend specific seasons and adjust the act as he saw fit, with due notification being place in the *Dublin Gazette*.

The Natural History Museum collection reveals that birds available at Dublin Markets in 1916 included teal, golden eye, gadwall and also in 1895 barnacle geese (c.f. The Barrington Collection).

A number of birds were conspicuous by their absence on the protected list – for example, the eagle, the heron and the kestrel – but the Secretary of State could add them to lists if he saw fit.

On fowlers (Kennedy, 1953).

Other locations where birds ended up included museums such as the Science and Art Museum, or private collections such as Barrington's – now in the Natural History Museum; some of the collections by Montgomery appear to have made it to the National Museum in Dublin (Kennedy, 1953).

Possibly the stone curlew in the National History Museum is the one referred to by Ussher and Warren, who state it was obtained on the North Bull in December 1884 and sent to the Dublin Museum (Ussher and Warren, 1900).

The spotted redshank in the National History Museum is possibly the one shot among a flock of common redshanks at the North Bull, in August 1890, by Mr. A. Rohu, and placed in the Science and Art Museum in Dublin (Ussher and Warren, 1900).

In lining its nest the tern favoured razor and cockles (Patten, C. J., 1899, 'The construction of the nest of the Little Tern (Sterna minuta)', *The Irish Naturalist*, 8(9), 189-197).

Birds of Ireland noted at Clontarf an osprey, shot in 1881; an eider duck, shot in 1869; the velvet scooter, shot in 1883; the surf-scooter, shot by E. Hanks in 1880; a sand grouse, killed in the migration of 1888; a stone curlew, shot in 1829, the black winged stint (obtained prior to 1837); bar tailed godwit, the sandwich tern, shot in the 1830s and 1840s; Sabine's gull, a great skua (preserved by Messrs William and Son, and then in Dublin Museum), Leache's fork-tailed petrel and a Kentish plover, killed with a stone.

More, Alexander, G., 1885, *A List of Irish Birds*, Dublin, Alex Thom & Co.

Barrington, R., 1900, *The Migration of Birds as Observed at Irish Lighthouses and Lightships*, Dublin, Edward Ponsoby.

On bird acts (Rikards, G., 1869, *The Statutes of the United Kingdom*, London, George E. Eyre). Kennedy (1953) noted that the last two snowy owls on the island were spotted in the winter of 1880-1881 and again in early 1884. In the 1960s the *Irish Press* estimated as many as six short eared owls were living on the island.

On 1896 bird act (Marchant, J.R. and Watkins, 1897, *Wild Birds Protection Acts, 1880-1896*, London, R.H. Porter).

On prosecution of the Reynolds brothers (my wife's surname) (Anon., 1897, November 6, 'Wild bird fowling', *The Irish Times*).

Freeman's Journal reader Henry McLaughlin Barnes notes the shooting of the 'marine cormorant' was 'quite accidental', but the tone suggests a self-effacing brag, rather than any legal concerns. He intended to have the 'corus marines' stuffed and presented to a museum (Anon., 1903, *Freeman's Journal*, p. 11).

On the Ibis (Kennedy, 1953).

On Divine (Anon., 1906, June 6, 'Trapping skylarks on the North Bull', *The Irish Times*, p. 2).

On 'crying evil' (Williams, A., 1908, 'Wild bird protection in Co. Dublin', *Irish Naturalist*, 17(6), pp. 119-122).

On the DSPCA (Anon., 1910, October 29, *Freeman's Journal*, p. 2.; Anon., 1908, September 29, 'Dundrum Licences', *Freeman's Journal*, p. 2).

On wanton slaughter (Anon., 1932, August 16, *Irish Independent*, p. 6).

20

The Crow's Nest

As you cross the wooden bridge on to the island, on your left-hand side you pass a small group of cottages. For the most part of the last two centuries these have constituted the coast guard station. In 1864, the coast guard had to draw water by cart on to the island although it was hoped that the Corporation might run out pipes to island as first reported in the *Waterworks Gazette*. A watchtower once existed in the early twentieth century, but was later demolished (it was probably damaged when the station was burned by the IRA as Ireland sought independence). The suitability of the coast guard station's position now seems curiously inappropriate – it has very little visibility of the waters surrounding the island. But when the coast guard was first built – at least as early as 1864 – the island was lower and smaller, and it would have had a clear view of the sea on all sides.

It is not clear what the living conditions were like for the coast guard, but morale may have been low because at times their vigilance was questioned. In 1874, a brig called the *Hampton* had its top gallant sail broken in a half gale. Laden with coal it knocked on a rock on the Bull Wall and commenced to fill. Captain McFall and one seaman were washed overboard and drowned. Seven more crew climbed into the fore topmast rigging, but the spar broke and they too were washed overboard. They hung on in an angry sea. Though only a short distance away, the coast guard made no attempt to rescue the crew, and were later criticised for not keeping a proper lookout and simply *not bothering* to do their job. In 1878, events surrounding the accidental drowning of John Lewis, who was found near the coast guard station, provoked the *Freeman's Journal's* into further complaints that the coast guards who were engaged in taking the body ashore did not make use of the means that were necessary to resuscitate life.

For the most part, however, records indicate nothing but gallantry, even if there certainly appears to have been a basic – if perhaps understandable – problem with visibility. In 1879, *The Alice Wood*, laden with 325 tonnes of coal, was stranded in heavy seas on the east side of the breakwater, short of the new lighthouse. Six of the vessel's crew had lashed themselves to the rigging – the sails themselves had already been carried away. Neither crew nor vessel was spotted until daybreak, but when they were, coast guard officer John Bynon and four others went to their assistance. After a boat rescue had proved ineffectual, the coast guard team climbed out on to the breakwater rocks with ropes to haul each crewmember to safety. (It is important to remember that the engineering of the Bull Wall did not remove the danger of the Bull Sands to shipping. Both the wall itself and, in particular, the submerged breakwater represented new shipping hazards. Numerous ships continued to collide with the sands after the wall's construction – a situation that only declined with the rise of steam ships.)

The 1911 census indicates the existence of a number of houses just past the wooden bridge, all owned by Lord Ardilaun – better known as Arthur Edward Guinness (great grandson of the brewer). Collectively, the occupants – mostly coast guard families – described themselves as either Church of England, Church of Ireland, Methodist or Roman Catholic. Interestingly, this tight-knit Christian community appears to have maintained a degree of religious harmony in the 'unidenominational' [sic] sermons of H.W. O'Dwell on the sands at the coast station. Perhaps such a dangerous occupation humbled in the face of nature did not allow for the luxury of schism.

In 1929, the coast guard cottages also hosted a pair of starlings. The chimneys were frequented by one starling in particular that was well known for its ability to mimic the curlew.

The Crow's Nest – Notes

They cottages had gardens used for growing vegetables.

In 1839, a coast guard officer James Gilbert appears to have been living at the address of Crab Lake (Gogarty, 2013). In 1800, the Ballast Board employed John Clements of Ringsend to build a lifeboat to be stationed at the Sheds in Clontarf. One was also moved from here to the Pigeon house in 1825 (De Courcy, 1996).

On waterworks (Anon., 1864, November 4, *The Irish Times*).

The sea scouts also had a home there from 1912; this building was demolished and rebuilt into a new scout hall in the late twentieth century.

In 1982, John Byrne was killed on the bridge when a stolen BMW driven by one Paul Boyle hit his own car on the bridge. Byrne had been driving with his wife Betty to collect their son from the sea scouts. Boyle got a mere three years penal servitude. Betty, who survived, had to be forcefully removed from the courtroom (Anon., 1982, December 1, *Irish Press*, p. 1).

In 1921, the Admiralty claimed £2,800 from Dublin County Council for the burning of the station; many other stations were also attacked (Anon., 1921, September 19, *Freeman's Journal*, p. 8). Knowles (1970) claims part of the station was burnt by the IRA.

The tower may have been, or may have been separate to, the watch house engraved by Samuel Templeton, who shows the dramatic landing of the crew of *The Edward*, wrecked on the Bull in November 1825. In addition to the dramatic events, the engraving shows a small wooden hut, a crane or winch, fishing nets and two small rowing boats stationed on the wall (NLI: PD HP (1825) 1).

Brig: a sailing vessel with two square-rigged masts.

On McFall (Anon., 1874, April 15, *Freeman's Journal*, p. 2.)

On coast guard flaws (Anon., 1874, April 14, 'Wreck of a Dublin Brig', *The Irish Times*, p. 6).

On Lewis (Anon., 1878, April 23, 'Fatal occurrence at Dollymount', *Freeman's Journal*, p. 7).

On the *Alice Wood* (Anon., 1879, November 22, 'Wreck of a vessel at the North Bull', *The Irish Times*).

Steamships were first introduced in 1816 and were dominant by 1860. But steam colliers did not appear until 1880 and overseas cargo continued to be carried by sail as late as 1883 (Daly, 2011).

In 1911, the first cottage belonged to two members of the Church of England, Eliza and William Humber. William was Chief Petty Officer of the coast guard. They had no children. House 2 also held a Royal Navy coast guard member, the English born Joseph Weber and his Scottish wife Catherine. Methodists, they had a daughter Rosa aged just 2. In house 3, Roman Catholics Mary and William Behan (coast guard) had four boys and one daughter. The two youngest boys were both under three. One child had died earlier. In house 4, James and Elizabeth Hemming had three sons and two daughters. The family were Methodist. James was also a coast guard member. House 5 was uninhabited. In house 6, Ellen Gore was visiting the Kennedys and their two daughters. Both Ella (15) and Sophie (12) were members of Church of Ireland, like their mother, and not Roman Catholic like their father, a retired coast guard officer. The four occupants of house 7, all Howards, had seven domestic servants (who were Church of Ireland and Roman Catholic). John was the golf club steward, and running 'the golf club hotel' seems to have necessitated five waiters (Julia and Mary Nolan, Patrick Hughes, Hannah Millea, Matilda Ripton), a kitchen maid (Teresa Salina), and a cook (Kate Hodgins). In House 8, Church of Ireland members Archibald and Lillian Hargrave had a son William aged 2. Archibald was a photographer.

On sermons (Anon., 1906, August 11, 'Clontarf open air meeting', *The Irish Times*, p. 8).

Religious aside, OSI maps indicate that at one stage Bull Island was in Clontarf Parish, while its islands were in Raheny. Various religious ceremonies have occurred over the years. In 1965, for example, the Jehovah's Witnesses held baptisms by immersion on the Bull (Anon., 1965, June 10, *Irish Press*, p. 11). In 1969, a fully clothed George Woodhouse (18) was baptised by immersion on Bull Island to make him a member of the Pentecostal Church (Anon., 1969, November 17, *Irish Press*, p. 4).

Starlings are known for their mimicry. Ones at the Royal Dublin could mimic the mistle thrush (apparently unknown in Ireland prior to 1808) and redshank (Kennedy, (1935; D'Arcy, G., 1999, *Ireland's Lost Birds*, Dublin, Four Courts Press).

21

Bathing Waters

In 1844, J. Fraser noted that the Bull Wall, or 'mole', afforded good views and good bathing at all times (though as now the exact location of the bathing depended on tides). However, bathing was not a new experience for the area brought on by the wall's construction, but an extension of an existing tradition.

In 1792, Clontarf is described by Daniel Beaufort as being crowded in the season for sea-bathing. The owners of many of the residences were eminent merchants and gentry. They possessed cottages, possibly thatched with the nearby common reed, which they let as 'summer residences and bathing lodges'. Bathing boxes, also known as bathing machines, were also established on the strand itself. Lady Morgan's memoirs recount how she raced her classmates to one, only to find a man asleep in it. Startled awake, he jumped from the box, jumped in a rowing boat and fled to sea.

In 1836, Charles Garfew and other landholders and inhabitants of the Sheds at Clontarf petitioned against a proposed railway line being built in their area. If, as proposed, steam engines were allowed to run along the strand the value of these residences would be greatly diminished. Clontarf would cease as a resort for sea-bathing and the railway would threaten cockle harvesting and oyster farming. Lord Vernon similarly testified that a railroad would destroy the bathing at Clontarf, the whole of the coast would be 'much injured'. His objections would be lessened only if he could be persuaded that the bathing would not be destroyed.

In 1836, Dollymount is also noted as a popular bathing place, where many people came to ride horses, walk and bathe. The railway demurred. At Dollymount there were only a score of houses, small summer cottages and a few public houses used by parties of pleasure. The area was little used for bathing, which in comparison to the south of the city may have been accurate to a certain extent. The strand that the new railway line would pass over was negatively described as 'waste strand'. However in 1837, Lewis again confirms the regional significance of Clontarf, which was much frequented by visitors from the north of Dublin for sea-bathing; and that consequently several neat cottages, and numerous pleasant villas and ornamented cottages had been built in the area. Landlords such as Vernon (and indeed Guinness) remained unconvinced of the merits of the railway on their land. And in the end they won out: the railway was not built along the coast but further inland. In the 1880s a charming horse-drawn coastal tram service was built (and later electrified) that ran until 1938. The tramcars were replaced by an ineffectual bus service to and from the Wooden Bridge. From there bathers could nonetheless quickly reach the sea.

Bathing Waters – Notes

Fraser, J., 1844, *Guide through Ireland,* Dublin, William Curry.

In 1818, 20,000 bathers were estimated to be present in Dublin bay on a good day (De Courcy, 1996).

Beaufort, D.A., 1792, *Memoir of a Map of Ireland: Illustrating the Topography of that Kingdom, and Containing a Short Account of Its Present State, Civil and Ecclesiastical; with a Complete Index to the Map,* London, Faden.

On gentry's residences (Mangnall, R., 1822, *Compendium of Geography,* London, Longman).

John Henry Campbell (1757-1829) painted one Clontarf cottage in watercolour, possibly around 1809 (Campbell, J.H., 1809?, 'A Cottage near Clontarf,' Dublin' National Library of Ireland).

Richard Kinsey of Clontarf left a bathing machine in his estate around 1829 (Anon., 1829, Handbill. Charles Sharpe, p. 1, RIA MR/17/F/10(52); an etching of Clontarf made by John Laporte in 1796 shows two such boxes (British Library King George III Topographical Collection, British Library).

Morgan mentions that the celebrated highwayman Barrington had been caught hiding out at the Sheds (Morgan, S., 1863, *Lady Morgan's Memoirs, Vol. 1,* Leipzig, Bernhard Tauchnitz).

The population of Clontarf around 1836 is given as 1,300, which would be all of Clontarf, not just the area around the Sheds. Twenty-nine manufacturing families were in the area, which was at one time serviced by various horse-drawn Omnibus, Jingles and Jaunting cars.

The sands were valued at £50 an acre (oysters, cockles, fishing, bathing, lead mines).

On railway threat (Anon., 1836, *Minutes of Evidence Taken Before the Committee on the Dublin and Drogheda Railway and Report*, London, Cox and Sons). The committee was chaired by Daniel O'Connell.

Horses were seemingly raced in 1849 (Anon., 1849, 'Sporting Intelligence', *Freeman's Journal*, p. 3).

Rental value of summer cottages was around £15.00-20.00.

The railway would have run in front of the sea-facing houses – a maximum distance of 20 yards.

22

Curley's Hole

In 1896, the father of a 21-year-old GPO clerk followed a few minutes after his son down to the Bull Wall. There was no sight of the young man – only his bicycle and clothes. After a search, the father was horrified to see his son's body lying in the water. In contrast to this drowning, a Eugene Smith of Cabra Park rescued one Callan on the city side of the Bull Wall in 1910. Of course, such events are not uncommon near water. But between the two possibilities of rescue and drowning, the island gained a degree of notoriety for swimming accidents at one 'location' in particular. And at it, as ebb follows flow, the unpalatable lesson that nature needs respect was taught and learned the hard way.

Curley's Hole was well known to locals, and appears to have taken its name, in one way or another, from the Curley family who lived in a cottage with a tin roof in the demesne of the Royal Dublin Golf Club. Located past the Royal, Curley's Hole may or may not have been Brophy's Hole, into which one Allingham jumped in 1864. His legs stuck deep in some mud at the bottom preventing him from rising. The coast guard rescued him, but his life was found to be 'quite extinct'.

Strictly speaking, the current at this location was not necessarily insurmountable – at least not for athletes. In 1887, a
famous distance runner had retrieved a man from the hole,
although resuscitation efforts – including brandy from the
coast guard an hour later – failed. But most people aren't athletes; in the same year, cooper Joseph Johnston stepped into
the water imploring his partner Higgins to come in and have
a wash together. He quickly weakened trying to swim against
the strong current and perished. A prescient local, Mr. Bayhan
of Clontarf, had warned Johnston to be wary – that the place
was dangerous. This was true and good advice. But stupidity
is deaf to advice and immune to common sense.

Like most of humanity, youth does not fare exceptionally
well on a scale of common sense, but it suffers from the additional problem of excessive bravery. In 1901, Kevin Quinn (17)
and three others went to bathe at Curley's Hole, which was
reported as 'a treacherous pool where the currents have been
responsible for many a drowning fatality'. Quinn soon got into
difficulty. A horrified James Spence swam to his assistance,
but soon became exhausted trying to drag his struggling companion to shallow water. Spence only just managed to escape
being dragged down with Quinn. The boy disappeared and
never rose.

An intrinsic part of the problem it seems was that the hole
had attractive warm water. However, this was accompanied
by a whirlpool current, one strong enough to noticeably tug
downwards at boats. Complicating matters, a strong ebb tide
could also be present. The hole reputedly even moved. For
the weak, then, it seems almost a given that drowning was
a distinct possibility. A few days after Kevin Quinn drowned
in 1901, one such weak swimmer, a 12-year-old epileptic boy

called Thomas Norris, attempted to bathe here. And again, as in Quinn's case, a witness (Joseph Ledwidge) was unable to save the boy from Curley's Hole. The boy's body was found three-quarters of a mile away (tides in the bay can be strong and carry quite a distance – in 1760, the bodies of two children from a Bull disaster were found across the bay at Irishtown).

The ensuing inquest revealed that nine or ten people had drowned at the spot 'in recent years'. The Port and Docks Board decided to mark the spot as dangerous and place a life buoy beside the notice board. This was more than a little belated. A letter to *The Irish Times* had first suggested putting a floating buoy at Curley's Hole in 1886, claiming that many had drowned there and that bodies were only recovered with difficulty. But even a buoy was not entirely effective. In 1905, William Weathers, a tailor by trade, drowned after entering water 50 yards from Curley's Hole marker. It was useless to refer again to the dangers of Curley's Hole, said the coroner: the authorities had done all they could.

Curley's Hole was said to be about half a mile past the island's Royal Golf Club, but it no longer appears to exist. The continued transformation of the island may have mitigated its appetite – by 1990, a 'dangerous for bathing sign' had receded 100 yards into the dunes. However, quite when the hole disappeared is unclear. As late as 1929, Gordon Brewster would caricature the inaction of both Dublin Corporation and the Port and Docks Board in a cartoon entitled 'The bathers' death trap at Dollymount'. Both authorities were shown sitting on their asses doing nothing. And it was still referenced as existing on 'the Dollymount Bull' by the poet Stringer in the 1940s.

By 1943 it was said to have been nearly filled up, but a new 10-feet deep and 'distinctly dangerous' hole had opened up near it. This unnamed hole is known to have claimed at least two victims. It too no longer appears to be present. Though fairly well understood, these forces of nature were never wilfully mastered or tamed. Like many who refused them respect, they simply disappeared. It is not clear if we will see them again.

Curley's Hole – Notes

On GPO clerk (Anon., 1896, July 21, 'Sad case of drowning', *The Irish Times*, p. 5).

The Curley family are also associated with 'The Stables', which was a walled enclosure within the Royal Dublin Golf Club, and which may have been opposite this treacherous location. Some sources suggest that the hole may have got its name from Patrick Curley, who was the grandfather of legendary Royal Dublin golfer Michael Birdie Moran. In 1910, Michael Curley was a golf club attendant at the Royal Dublin.

On Allingham (Anon., 1864, October 1, *Freeman's Journal*, p. 4).

On Johnston (Anon., 1887, July 11, 'Fatal bathing accident at Dollymount', *The Irish Times*).

The currents around the bay could take a body far and wide. In 1760, a 'wherry' from Dungarvan perished near the Bull and the bodies of two children were later washed up in Irishtown (Anon., 1760, February 29, *Belfast Newsletter*, p. 2).

On Quinn (Anon., 1901, July 20, 'Boy Drowned at Dollymount', *The Irish Times*).

On ebb tide (Anon., 1901, July 22, *Freeman's Journal*, p. 3).

On letter (Anon., 1886, August 18, 'Caution of bathers', *The Irish Times* – the letter was signed *Pro Utilitate Hominum*)

Weather's companion – James George – survived. Dr. Stoker (no prizes for guessing who he was related to) and Dr. Lermon tried unsuccessfully to resuscitate Weathers.

On the coroner (Anon., 1905, July 18, 'Drowned in Curley's Hole', *Irish Independent*, p. 6).

In 1930, Frederick Treacy was reported as having drowned at Curley's Hole while his uncle played golf nearby (Anon., 1930, September 8, 'Tragedy at Curley's Hole, Dollymount', *Irish Independent*, p. 9)

Knowles suggests Curley's Hole may have got its name from one Dyke Curley (Knowles, 1970); MyIntyre states that the hole got its name after a member of the Curley family was drowned with his horse (McIntyre, 1987).

On receding signs (Anon., 1990, October 23, *Irish Press*, p. 29).

On cartoon (Brewster, G., 1929, September 21, 'The bathers' death trap at Dollymount', The Gordon Brewster Collection, National Library of Ireland).

'For the love of your country and the good of your soul / Be aware, take care, don't touch Curley's Hole (Jane Stringer in Lynch, 2007).

On new hole (Anon., 1943, *Irish Independent*, p. 4).

23

Found Drowned

Bull Island is teeming with life that is endlessly fascinating. But the presence of life is not always obvious. Local historian Denis McIntyre goes further. The first-time visitor, he states, has the impression of something barren, insignificant, weed-infested, windswept and of a bleak wilderness of sand. The same impression is probably true for many of the people who visit it for the last time.

On a Saturday in 1863, the body of a female, name unknown, was found washed on to the strand at the North Bull. She looked about 24. She had on a dark dress, white cotton stockings and laced leather boots. In contrast to drowned swimmers, she shared what many bay suicides have in common: she was dressed. In 1899, a clean-shaven man, name unknown, was also found drowned. The forty-something was dressed in tweed coat and trousers, a couple of cotton shirts and a pair of new boots. In his pockets were a pair of scissors and a tailor's thimble. Three days earlier the drowned man had told one Robinson that he wanted to kill himself. Robinson had given the man money with instructions to get himself a drink. This initially seemed to have worked. But the clean-shaven man later returned, walked into sea near the point of the Bull Wall, and disappeared. An onlooker, Charles Ryan, nearly drowned during a failed rescue attempt. In 1902, the body of a respectably dressed man in his late fifties was also found in the water near the North Bull. Five-foot, nine-inches tall, he remained unidentified.

Walking on the strand on 22 August 1899, Private John Kane of the Kings Own Yorkshire Light Infantry turned and shook the hand of his companion James Walker. 'Goodbye Walker,' he said, shooting himself in the head with the gun in his free hand. The story of the doubtlessly traumatised Walker may have been hard to believe: however supporting letters were found on Kane's body, in which Kane had threatened to kill himself and a woman in Liverpool also named Kane. For some, then, there exists a profound sense of both isolation and unrelenting emptiness on the island (also exploited by those who push for its development), which matches their mental condition. Though, of course, not all suicide attempts were successful.

This presented its own unique problems for such desperate souls because suicide was illegal (society's prejudices are embodied in its laws). In 1910, golf club attendant Michael Curley rescued a Mrs Kate Gavan. Curley had found Gavan lying on her face in two or three feet of water. After artificial respiration and a spell in hospital Gavan found herself on trial at Raheny Petty Sessions, charged with attempted suicide. After her husband testified she had no signs of insanity but that she had been weak from an operation, Magistrates directed that Gavan should have good future behaviour – and that her husband should provide proper medical care.

Found Drowned – Notes

On first impressions (McIntyre, 1987).

On woman's body (Anon., 1863, August 17, 'Found drowned', *The Irish Times*, p. 2).

On clean-shaven man (Anon., 1899, August 18, 'Supposed suicide', *The Irish Times*).

On unidentified body (Anon., 1902, September 26, 'Found Drowned', *The Irish Times*).

On Private Kane (Anon., 1899, August 24, 'The late suicides at the North Bull', *The Irish Times*, p. 7).

There is educated guesswork here. In 1908, an insomniac teacher, Francis Hughes, was found drowned 300 yards from the coast guard station. His cap, bicycle, coat and silver watch and gold chain were found at the wall. He left his house at 8.00 pm. A lot here suggests that he might have killed himself, though of course he could have had a traumatic health event, or accidentally drowned. Even murder can't be ruled out. The same caveats apply to some of the other cases. What can be said for certain though is that the North Bull Wall was a popular place for life's disillusioned (Anon., 1908, May 8, *Freeman's Journal*, p. 5).

24

The Actor

Mid-summer, in blazing sun, I am out on my crutches heading towards the Bull Wall. Sadhbh is on her pink scooter and zooms ahead. She stops near a bench with a grey man, who makes pleasant talk with her. I catch up and sit down with them. A newspaper hangs from his pocket. He is gaunt, shadowed and perhaps homeless. For a while I think he might even be blind.

As Sadhbh scoots up and down, we speak of the weather, my cast, of Clontarf Island. He tells me that he once was an actor. He mesmerises with accounts of Burton and the great actors and speaks of depression and suicide. He tells how even an actor can't keep pretending. 'It's too tiring.'

25

'You Have Insulted Us'

For everything that society declares to be an act of insanity, it appears to have several more dubious activities that it actively encourages. The most notable activity that comes to mind with respect to the Bull, however, had fallen out of fashion in Dublin by the time of the wall's construction in 1820. By then the once accepted practice of duelling was not only illegal, but very much on the wane. If truth be told, even the papers seemed a little bored with it.

Yet in 1835, after James Haire accused J.J. Murphy of having deceived a court, the two men met on Bull Island to settle their differences. The first bullets missed both men. A second round ensued ('you have insulted us, we must have a second shot'). These shots were again without effect. There were no third shots. Haire was removed by his compatriot – without remark or explanation – but probably under some prior arrangement between the two hostile parties. This remarkably ill-advised way of coming to a mutually beneficial agreement fell under what the newspapers called 'An Affair of Honour'.

Typically, 'An Affair of Honour' (or pig-headed stupidity) took place under certain codes or rules of conduct, often ones published in books. The exact rules to be implemented would have been further negotiated by each protagonist's 'second'. These friends would also have tried to negotiate an amicable settlement or supplied more guns – when their friend – as was often the case – missed. In 1839, one Mr. Flynn therefore engaged a Mr. O'Hara after the latter used an expression he found personally offensive. Having shot at each other without effect second pistols were called for, but before anything could happen the decidedly inaccurate Flynn shot himself in the thigh, ending the duel. Though dangerous, the mortality rate was low for such duels. And in Flynn's case nineteenth century medicine may have given him something more to worry about than a mere verbal insult.

That such conflict was often farcical and somewhat pathetic seems clear from those writing at the time. In 1839, a story in *The Dublin University Magazine*, 'The Confessions of Harry Lorrequer', deftly caricatures the nature of duelling on Bull Island. Drunk one night on sherry and champagne, Lorrequer had made the error of instantly forgetting his proposal of marriage to the sister-in-law of one Mark Anthony Fitzpatrick, who got most upset and a duel was promptly arranged. At eight the next morning, Lorrequer found himself on Bull Island waiting with his friend Curzon and a doctor in a chilly rain and raw fog. They waited in vain. Fitzpatrick, unable to come, sent his friend O'Gorman, who offered to take his place if Lorrequer would waive etiquette. When the gracious offer was declined, O'Gorman offered a second option. O'Gorman explained that Fitzpatrick, no coward, had actually been slung in the debtor's prison. If Lorrequer could help bail Fitzpatrick, then Fitzpatrick would gladly come and shoot Lorrequer the next morning . . .

Mocked or not, the practice continued for another while yet. In 1840, Hercules McDonald (and how could you not duel with a name like that?) had just missed blowing Joseph Griffith's head off when the Gardaí – somewhat conveniently tipped off – arrested all parties ('a lady was the cause of the meeting'). In 1847, following a political dispute in the boxes of the Theatre Royal, we find that one Barnet Barry and Englishman Welland Price similarly exchanged shots. Price was wounded in the hip and there once again the farce ended.

By 1890, we find a passing quip in *The Irish Times* about the possibility of duels being held again on the North Bull, which seems to indicate that they were now very much a thing of the past. By this time personal honour was a tarnished commodity. It was no longer worth fighting over, and aggressive machismo was directed into shooting at target boards – and of course birds – via organisations such as the Bull's Irish Rifle Association. It had been formed around 1867 (but existed informally prior to then along with archery), and while most people were forbidden to shoot, and though shooting was strictly for the elite (with the Lord Lieutenant a frequent attender), all-day competitions were both national and international. Local and international newspapers keenly reported shots on target. If the weather was favourable large crowds were in attendance.

Competitors often practiced on snipe and game like pheasants (pigeon shooting – with real pigeons – had also occurred, although numbers were deemed insufficient). Yet for the annual prize shooting match they used target boards at a distance of between 600 and 1,000 yards. The use of target boards was understandable: on such occasions birds disappeared early and did not show themselves until long after the disturbance had ceased. Doubtless the military band (much in fashion) wouldn't have helped either.

In 1875, an unprecedented 30,000 people jostled to see America take on Ireland, leading to marksmen being jostled as they tried to shoot and people being crushed on the wooden bridge. Such chaotic scenes raised complaints but appear to have been tolerated; shooting was widely seen by people as both manly and in the nation's military interests – at least until the Great War. Sometimes society only learns the hard way.

'You Have Insulted Us' – Notes

On Haire and Murphy (Anon., 1835, June 30, *Belfast Newsletter*, p. 4).

On Flynn (Anon., 1839, June 7, *Belfast Newsletter*, p. 4).

On Lorrequer (Anon., 1839, *The Dublin University Magazine*, vol. 14).

On McDonald (Anon., 1840, January 28, *Freeman's Journal*, p. 2).

On Price (Anon., 1847, January 26, *Belfast Newsletter*, p. 4).

On duel quip (Anon., 1890, January 18, 'The coming storm! A Breezy Session', *The Irish Times*, p. 4).

A Major Leech, who published a rifle manual, was one of the major figures on the scene (Anon., 1867, June 17, *Freeman's Journal*, p. 6).

On shooting restrictions (Anon., 1867, July 6, 'How to shoot', *The Nation*, p. 9).

On Lord Lieutenant (Anon., 1869, June 24, *Freeman's Journal*, p. 4).

Archery may also have featured in competitions: strong wind ruled out an archery fete in 1862.

There may have been a clubhouse of sorts. In 1875 a large wooden house was for sale on the shooting grounds (Anon., 1875, July 7, *The Irish Times*).

On pigeons (Anon., 1874, June 10, *Freeman's Journal*, p. 3).

The prize meeting at Dollymount was by permission of the Earl of Howth and J. C. Venables Vernon.

On shooting (Anon., 1862, October 2, 'Annual Prize Shooting Match'. *The Irish Times*, p. 4). This article also suggests that the Bull could be used for athletics. Other groups to frequent the island for athletic purposes would include the Irish Vegetarian Society's athletic section (1907) and the Royal Irish Constabulary's Depot Cycling Club (1905) who enjoyed heading to the wall 'for a dip in the briny'.

On crush (Lynch, 2007).

26

Sanctuary

In 1914, while flying over the island, a brent goose was unfortunate enough to meet a golf ball in full flight. It was killed stone dead – an event sufficiently interesting internationally to make the French weekly *Le Chenil*. But during the Great War of 1914–1918, the birds enjoyed a brief respite from accidental golf shots and other more mischievous human pastimes, such as trapping. Having commandeered the island, the military now strictly controlled access to it. And despite firing practice at the Royal Golf Club, the ISPB noted that 'terneries' at the North Bull were flourishing. (The disruption of war also meant that trafficking in songbirds was diminishing.)

In 1917, 12 members of the Dublin Naturalists' Field Club gained access to the island and luncheoned in the hollows past the army huts 'on rich botanical ground carpeted with the sea milk wort' among other items including pyramidal orchids. In the air, six spotted burnets and the silver-washed fritillary butterfly were also present, hovering over yellow ragweed and sea bent. In 1918, the clouded yellow butterfly was also among one of the more interesting finds spotted on the 'sand hills' of the North Bull, along with dancing grayling and various moths.

After the hatching of the Irish state, the spring of 1927 saw barrister and Senator Samuel Lombard Brown introduce a bill to prohibit the use of bird-lime (an adhesive substance used in trapping birds), maimed decoy-birds, and the taking of eggs from the lapwing. It passed in the Dáil but was rejected in the Senate by 40 votes to 22, the legislation being notably opposed by the Farmers' Party. Ironically, the inability of the house to pass even a modicum of protection for the birds resulted in a surge of public agitation. Seizing on this mood for action, Brown and others such as Charles Moffat re-drafted the bill. They recoded existing legislation, added greater provisions and reintroduced it at what was judged the optimal time for it to pass. As such, the *Wild Birds Protection Act* eventually came into force in 1930 (though the bill was fought at every stage). Building quickly on this success, the Irish Society for the Protection of Birds (founded in 1904) further successfully petitioned the city to make the island a bird sanctuary, which it duly did in 1931. Although the statute books did not prevent game birds from being hunted, the island had also passed into the hands of Rev. Bishop Plunkett (a nephew of Guinness), who by 1932 had forbidden game from being hunted.

When Bull Island was declared a bird sanctuary, birds were reported as being noticeably tamer. By 1935, many species had increased in numbers, particularly the pintail and the shoveler. Over the catastrophic arctic winter of 1947, fieldfares could feed with some safety on the island. By 1954, a letter to the *Southern Star* describes the island as being famous abroad for its wild bird life. Nothing seemed impossible. The white throat was spotted for the first time in 1955. And in

1965, the practically extinct Irish crane caused understandable excitement by apparently appearing on the North Bull – but this wishful sighting turned out to be a pelican recently escaped from Dublin Zoo.

The preservation of the island occurred in an era where a degree of social change was also impacting positively on bird life. By 1931, the *Irish Independent* reported that the keeping of birds in small cages had been largely abandoned. Song birds had also increased in gardens. Similarly, shooting swans declined around the 1940s, after public outrage concerning their use in the manufacture of women's powder puffs (already, by 1908, a flying swan at Dollymount was described as a rare spectacle). This followed earlier campaigns by the Royal Society of the Protection of Birds against the wearing of egret and heron feathers in hats.

For all that, the danger to birds remained very much alive. Though better protected by domestic and international legislation, systematic robbery had made eggs rarer and more collectible. In 1932, the *Irish Independent* complained of 'the unceasing efforts of English dealers to rob our fields of the song birds that British law forbids them to capture in their own land, and the raids that unscrupulous wholesale collectors and their agents (almost invariably from overseas) endeavour to make on the known breeding haunts of our rarest birds, with a view to making a clean sweep of the eggs' (unacknowledged was Irish complicity in failing to protect the environment – even the ornithologist Ussher had been a notorious egg collector). And despite the island's apparent success, Kennedy noted in 1953 that the spread of bungalows and other building in the locality had driven away the corn bunting and tree sparrows.

By 1955, further threats meant that the ISPB were still pleading that the island be preserved as an open air living museum. Old problems remained unresolved. By 1970, for example, it was fully recognised that threats to Bull Island included the continued inland use of pesticides, which had brought falcons to the point of extinction. And in 1986, the reason for the little tern being wiped out on Bull Island was under scrutiny, with unleashed dogs suspected as a major disrupting factor (in 1891, by contrast, there were some thirty nests). The long-term future was looking uncertain too. Each spring brent geese, 'the darlings of the Bull', had migrated from their wintering grounds at Bull Island, via Iceland and Greenland to Bathurst Island in the Canadian Arctic Archipelago, a wearisome journey. Numbering 16,000 in 1973, their numbers had dropped to 13,000 by 1984. In 1989, climatologists warned that the greenhouse effect could lead to the diminishment of breeding grounds of brent geese in the Arctic Circle. 'We will miss the brent geese,' wrote the *Irish Press*.

And yet for those geese who continue to make their long migration, the island, however compromised, still remains a vital sanctuary.

Sanctuary – Notes

On goose meets golf ball (Anon., 1914, February 26, *Le Chenile*, p. 100).

Even bathing at the wall was banned (Anon., 1915, June 25, *Freeman's Journal*, p. 2).

On flourishing Terneries (Anon., 1917, January 20, *Freeman's Journal*, p.,15). The ISPB had earlier placed a watcher on the Shelly Bank to protect the lesser tern from people raiding their nests and helped protect the terns at Malahide Island (Williams, A., 1908).

On songbird trafficking (Anon., 1918, June 7, 'City and District', *Freeman's Journal*, p. 4).

The Field Club also noted knotted spurrey, sand pansy, yellow worth, centaury.

On butterflies (Walker, F.H., 1921, 'Lepidoptera at Dollymount, Co. Dublin', *The Irish Naturalist*, 30(5), pp. 62-63). Other interested lepidoptera parties included Kenneth Bond and microlepidopterist Henry Heal, who visited the saltmarsh in 1983 and removed plants for breeding the specimens therein (Bond, K., 1987, 'Henry Heal (1920-1986) Microlepidopterist', *The Irish Naturalists' Journal*, 22(6), 218).

On Dáil vote (Moffat, C. B., 1931, 'Our advance in bird protection', *The Irish Naturalists' Journal*, 3(12), pp. 251-254).

On opposing legislation (Anon., 1927, May 12, 'Protecting our wild birds', *Irish Independent*, p. 8).

Precedent for the creation of the sanctuary included earlier protection for Phoenix Park and St. Stephens Green.

One of the motives for the sanctuary's foundation was educational. In 1926, for example, Kennedy could hope that boys robbing nests could be taught to be observers not just collectors (Anon., 1926, March 25, 'Bird Sanctuaries', *Irish Independent*, p. 6).

On fieldfares (Kennedy, 1953).

On being famous for birdlife (Anon., 1954, January 9, *Southern Star*, p. 4).

On white throat (Odlum, W. P., 1955, 'Bird notes from the Bull Island, Dublin'. *The Irish Naturalists' Journal*, 11(11), 309).

In another famous case of mistaken identity in 1930, a penguin turned out to be a great northern diver (Kennedy, 1953).

On small cages (Anon., 1932, May 11, 'Irish Birds never better protected', *Irish Independent*, p. 7).

On increase in song birds (Anon., 1931, May 6, 'Good effect of recent act', *Irish Independent*, p. 2).

On powder puffs (Anon., 1946, *Irish Independent*, p. 8).

The swan had escaped from St Anne's; to add to the drama, some boys chasing it in a boat capsized.

Bird Legislation in Northern Ireland banned illegally sourced imports, thus protecting song birds etc. from being exported to Northern Ireland from the south (Moffat, C.B., 1931, 'Our advance in bird protection', *The Irish Naturalists' Journal*, 3(12), pp. 251-254).

On bird protection (Anon., 1932, May 11, 'The Protection of Birds', *The Irish Times*, p. 4).

On a living museum (M.P.H.K., 1957, 'Irish Society for the Protection of Birds, Report for 1955', *The Irish Naturalists' Journal*, 12 (7), 204).

On pesticides (Anon., 1970, *Irish Press*, p. 3).

On wiped out tern (Anon., 1986, December 24, 'Self-stirring teapot', *Irish Press*, p. 3; Pattern, C.J., 1899, 'The construction of the nest of the Little Tern (Sterna minuta)', *The Irish Naturalist*, 8(9), 189-197).

On Bull darlings (McIntyre, 1987).

On geese numbers (Anon., 1984, May 3, 'Ecologists follow geese to midnight sun', *New Scientist*, p. 9).

On missing the geese (Anon., 1989, January 7, 'Temperate zone', *Irish Press*, p. 17).

27

A&E

When I had my cast removed it was discovered that I had developed deep-veined thrombosis. A clot in my leg could break off at any time, go to my brain or lungs, and kill me. I spent the night in A&E, with morbid thoughts for company. In the morning I was placed on a warfin treatment program. Rat poison would be used to thin my blood and prevent further clots, joked the doctor. With luck, the existing clot would disappear by itself. A&E is an unlikely temple for self-reflection. How fragile life is. In 1953, P.G. Kennedy wrote that telephone wires over the bridge resulted in many flying casualties. On one occasion he picked up a dead dunlin and put it his pocket. Later that night he found it to be alive. The next morning he released it.

A&E – Notes

Dunlin are also noted as present in Ussher and Warren (1900).

28

The Fog

At times fog obscures the island and also the sea. In 1773, the *Happy Return* was wrecked during thick fog. In 1879, a steamer, *The Neptune,* came ashore during thick fog that had lasted five days. By 1885, fog bells would ring four times every 30 seconds. With modern lighting the onshore fog is less threatening and seems less common, but before modern street lighting it was sometimes possible to even pass a best friend without recognition. The fog was described as thick, nasty and dangerous. In the scorching heat of July a sun fog can even rise and draw a veil over the island. People fade and disappear like ghosts – as if they had never existed. Sometimes disorienting apparitions appear. In 1917, the Dublin Naturalists Field Club collectively witnessed the mirage of an archipelago of rocky islets rise from the sea, through heat haze and drifting sea mist.

For this, and other obvious reasons, Bull Island is overlooked by lighthouses, such as the Green Bailey, which now marks the northern entrance to Dublin Bay and dates to 1814. Prior to its construction, a much higher cottage lighthouse with a coal-burning beacon existed from around 1667. It was later abandoned – far too often it was shrouded in fog. However, for those on the Bull sands, the most notable lighthouse is the Poolbeg Lighthouse. This stands on the end of the Southern Bull Wall and can be seen from much of the island. The Southern Bull Wall was originally built south of a shallow depth of water known as the Poolbeg, so the candle-lit lighthouse designed by John Smyth in 1767 came to be known as the Poolbeg Lighthouse.

Prior to 1880, a small 'wooden perch' had been erected at the end of the North Bull, though the Commissioners of Lights had argued for a stone beacon. This was declined by the then 'Trinity Board', who thought the lighthouse more useful to shipping. In any event, the Green Lighthouse was not enough to save the *Charles Bal*. This vessel had famously survived the pumice and ash of the volcanic eruption of Krakatoa in 1883, but came ashore on the North Bull in 1888. Ditto for the yacht '98' that lost its keel on the breakwater. It promptly sank forcing its occupants to swim to shore. Reasons for continued mishaps varied, but were usually comprehensible. For example, in the case of the *Snowdon*, which went aground in 1904, its steering had become deranged. But not everything finds a ready explanation. In 1906, the body of an unidentified artisan, wearing a dark serge jacket, black corduroy trousers, striped shirt and strong nailed boots, was found floating at the lighthouse. In his pockets were a small leather purse, two small keys and a penknife.

Further out to sea there is a second green lighthouse, called the North Bank Lighthouse. On a low tide you can see that it is firmly attached to the bed of the bay with six feet of pillars. It is two stories tall, and capped with a railed balcony and cubed light box, with a pointed roof. Like the other lighthouses, this too has a fog bell. At one time each light-house's bell made a different sound. Poolbeg had a mournful, two-note foghorn; the Bailey a deep throated roar; and further out to sea, cannon was fired from guns at the Kish Lightship. The sound travelled most clearly in the fog when traffic was almost at a standstill. To the historian Knowles, they sounded like a parody of the Sugar Plum Fairy.

The Fog – Notes

On the Happy Return (Brady, K., 2008, p. 222).

On the Neptune (Anon., 1879, December 11, 'A Steamer ashore on the North Bull', *Freeman's Journal*, p. 4).

On fog bells (Anon., 1885, October 23, *Freeman's Journal*, p. 8).

On dangerous, nasty, fog (Knowles, 1970).

In 1967, the hapless John Quirk came off his motorcycle in one such fog (Anon., 1964, November 10, *Irish Press*, p. 1).

On a mirage (Anon., 1917, 'Irish societies', *The Irish Naturalist*, 26(10), pp. 166-168).

The beacon couldn't save the *William Packet*, wrecked in 1696, with the loss of 80 lives and Brigadier Fitzpatrick, now buried in St. Patricks Cathedral. On maps of Howth we also find 'The candlesticks', which refer to a view of the Bailey from the shore through two pointed rocks known as 'The Needles'. But see also Candlestick Bay as described by De Courcy (1996).

The wall from the pigeon house to the lighthouse was referred to as the 'mole', probably a corruption of *môle* for jetty (Wright, G.N., 1825, *A Historical Guide to the City of Dublin, 2nd Edition*, London, Baldwin, Cradock and Joy).

On Smyth (Cox, R.C. and Gould, M.H., 1988, *Civil Engineering Ireland*, London, Thomas Telford). In the nineteenth century, numerous floating lighthouse ships, typically named after seabirds, also existed. Of the more well known, *The Kittiwake* was bought by Dublin's Harry Crosbie in 2010, so that it could be turned into a café. Another, *The Albatross*, was painted luminous and moored in Scotsman's bay for Dorothy Cross's art work 'Ghost Ship'. *The Guillemot* was sunk by a German U-boat.

On a wooden perch (Anon., 1872, February 16, *The Irish Times*).

On the *Charles Bal* (Anon., 1888, December 14, 'The Charles Bal', *The Irish Times)*.

On the *Snowdon* (Anon., 1904, December 10, 'Steamer delayed in the Liffey', *The Irish Times*. p. 5).

On the artisan (Anon., 1906, August 15, 'Dublin and District', *Irish Independent*, p. 6).

In 1839, a number of buoys were further placed on the 'spit' of the North Bull to work in tandem with this and other lighthouses, the outer one being known simply as the 'Spit Buoy' (Norie, J.W., 1839, *The New British Channel Pilot, Containing Sailing Directions from London to Liverpool*, London, Navigation Warehouse). There were also red buoys on the south side, and black ones on the north, once known as watermarks.

On a parody of the Sugar Plum Fairy (Knowles, 1970).

29

Fishing in the Underworld

Under the fog, beneath the water, lies a silent underworld. It is not so much inhabited by floating bodies as by the thick-lipped grey mullet, flounder, and the common goby, which spends part of its life cycle in the upper dykes and channels of the marsh. Also found in these waters at times are fairy shrimp, moon jellyfish and seahorses.

In 1800, Leonard MacNally noted that fishing and drift netting was prohibited at Clontarf Island without written consent – six months imprisonment and forfeiture of nets being the consequences for those who transgressed these laws. In 1818, records show that for three months after Michaelmas (September 29), a much prized variety of herrings – supposedly peculiar to Dublin – appeared in Dublin Bay. Dublin Bay herring had a sweet nutty flavour and were smaller, firmer and less oily than the common kind. And they had a deep and vivid green on their backs.

On the surface, all seemed fairly mundane in the world of nineteenth century Dublin fishing. However, evidence of an unexplained environmental change began to be remarked upon: sprat was no longer seen in the markets, though in the

time of John Rutty (1698-1775), it was taken in the Liffey between the city and further inland at Island Bridge. What at
first seemed only to be an oddity soon gave way to graver concerns. Over the next decades, writers of reports complained
that the Liffey was adulterated with noxious and deleteri-
ous substances that were 'most destructive to the fishery'.
The sources of the toxins that frequently flowed out into the
bay and toward the Bull were numerous: gas works, brewer-
ies, vitriol manufacturers, a sal ammoniac factory, lime from
the skinners and Henry's factory (whatever that discharged).
Salmon would 'go mad and jump out upon the banks' when
they encountered 'poisonous matter' at the Jones Chemical
Works on Watling Street. Some attempts to rectify matters
were made. In 1838, for example, following representations
regarding fisheries, Crosthwaite's chemical factory ceased to
dump directly into the river. But other factors were also at play
in devastating fish stock.

The general decline in fish stock was perceived to have
commenced post-1800. Aside from pollution, close season
fishing, rivers blocked by mills (flouting a law requiring 24
hours free passage of water, without which spawning fish
were crushed in mill wheels), damage via spearing with the
gaff (a stick with barbed spear or hook), and improvements
in fishing technology were all identified as contributing factors. Otters, seals and porpoises were fingered as competitive
pressures.

By 1844, a Scotsman, William Campbell arrived to fish
on the Bull. Campbell had long fished in Ireland and leased
and managed fisheries. He and his teams were proficient in
ever evolving types of commercial fishing technology, such as
stake nets and seine nets. Campbell was the first person to

bring the bag net to the area. Dublin waters were shallow and the bag net could fish in 60 feet of water, missing little. And unlike most others, he fished early in a season that spanned from February to August. Campbell thought the season should even be extended for bag nets. Doubtless because of the quantities he was capable of catching, he had earlier been driven from the village of Ringsend, on the south side of the bay. His nets had been torn by locals.

On the Bull, Campbell caught 70 salmon with the bag net. In calm weather, Campbell could also catch 'weak fish' at Crab Lake. With an easterly or southeasterly gale, he could also catch a large 'abundance of fish, with sea lice on them'. These only had a small amount of pea or milt (seminal fluid), suggestive of a successful return from nearby spawning grounds; salmon typically headed up the Tolka, or to edges of the Liffey to spawn at Lucan or the Strawberry Beds.

As noted, close season fishing, salmon number decline, and the illegitimate use of certain nets were already a significant source of concern in Dublin at this point. But records specifically indicate that Campbell was not interfered with on the Bull. An advert of 1845 also shows one 'Mr. Camul' offering to supply crimped salmon (salmon boiled in sea water) 'as usual' from stake nets at the north Bull. Campbell was certainly not alone. A court case of 1844 convicted one Clemens of setting up a bag net next to Mr. Worthington's – a tenant of Vernon (a new fishing act meant that only land owners adjacent to the sea had the right to use fixed nets). Similarly, in 1847 the *Success,* a fishing smack from Wicklow, shored on the Bull; its crew were saved but its nets lost, suggesting that they may also have been fishing nearby. The Bull appears to have been unable to cater to Campbell's commercial needs.

The Scotsman soon gave up in favour of fishing the Liffey. He quickly netted 800 salmon in one haul (a remarkable number given the supposed pollution; the entire bay catch was tallied at between 5,000–7,000 salmon) before once again having his nets cut.

For all that, Campbell argued that the total bay catch could be sustainably augmented to 50,000 if the river were protected, passes made over the weirs and noxious substances not discharged into the water. Others also argued for the close season to be extended. And that extensions be made for anglers, who didn't catch much, but who would then have a greater interest in protecting the river. The Bull itself appears to have had – at least temporarily – some level of fish stocks remaining. An 1875 reference in *The Irish Times* speaks of plaice abounding at the sands of the North Bull. Yet by 1919, trawlers would be banned from the bay, and inshore fishermen would complain that ring fishing had devastated fish stocks.

Fishing in the Underworld – Notes

Mullet were in the bay in large quantities in 1844 (Anon., 1846, *Reports from Commissioners, Vol. XXII*, London, Clowes and Sons).

On types of fish (Anon., 1971, February 1, 'Bull Island', *The Irish Times*).

MacNally, L., 1818, *The Justice of the peace for Ireland: Containing the authorities and duties of that officer*, Dublin, H. Fitzpatrick).

On sprat (Wartburton, J., Whitelaw, J. and Walsh, R., 1818).

On toxins (Anon., 1846, *Reports from Commissioners, Vol. XXII*, London, Clowes and Sons). Restrictions against tanneries and others dumping substances in the Liffey that might harm salmon go back to at least 1466 (De Courcy, 1996).

Campbell was licensed to do so by the city. It appears to have acquired the rights from Vernon around 1820 (De Courcy, 1996).

In 1844, 11 crews of up to ten men fished the bay with seine nets, including one Langan from Clontarf.

Around 1825, with the arrival of noisy steamers in the bay, frightened salmon would jump out of the water and on to the banks, but then quickly became habituated to the noise (Anon., 1846, *Reports from Commissioners, vol. XXII*, London, Clowes and Sons).

Unlike around 1700, salmon was no longer considered a food of the poor; unsuccessful attempts were made to track the fish using silver wire (Anon., 1846, *Reports from Commissioners, Vol. XXII*, London, Clowes and Sons).

On crimped salmon (Anon., 1845, February 17, *Freeman's Journal*, p. 1).

On the court case (Anon., 1844, April 9, *Freeman's Journal*, p. 3).

On the success (Anon., 1847, December 21, *Belfast Newsletter*, p. 2).

On plaice (Anon., 1875, November 18, *The Irish Times*).

On ring fishing (Anon., 1919, August 23, *Weekly Irish Times*). In the nineteenth century fishermen began to look outside the bay for fish and ports such as Howth would dominate at the expense of others such as Clontarf (c.f. De Courcy, 1996).

30

Lost and Found

While most Dubliners have traditionally seen nature as a bountiful and limitless resource, it must be said in their defence that at times they applied this philosophy equally to the belongings of their neighbours – especially those that came from the sea.

As far back as 1745 we find that Lord Howth jailed tenants for plundering ships recently wrecked on the Bull. This was not a deterrence. In 1756, we also find complaints of plundering by 'inhuman villains'. A ship 'lately stranded' on the Bull was stripped in such a manner that nothing was left. The villains carried their rapaciousness so far as to deprive the captain of a pair of his own blankets, which he himself was endeavouring to save from the wreck. Similarly, Denis Sheridan was charged with plundering a wreck in 1801. And John and Margaret Mitchel were charged with plundering fire arms on the Bull from the *Premier* in 1855.

The possibility of plundering meant that when the *Lark* from Philadelphia drove ashore near Sutton in 1757, guards were put in place to prevent the plundering of its flour. And sometimes, as with the beached *Speculation* in 1787, insurance companies placed such guards. Further protection came from the military. Gunfire from the South Wall Battery successfully deterred a boat from Dun Laoghaire from plundering a wreck in 1799. Actual salvage rights to various wrecks in the area were claimed by the Vernon Estate, so local parties also rushed to secure the wrecks. In 1766, for example, a sloop called the *Luch*, laden with porter, hops, gunpowder and saltpetre, struck the Bull. Thomas Harrison, the surveyor of Clontarf, was actively credited with helping save a great part of the cargo.

Most items had a reuse value. Vessels stranded on the North Bull that were in good order were put back to sea at the first opportunity. In 1790, for example, a vessel from Jamaica laden with sugar and mahogany was refloated with very little damage. On the other hand, wrecks could be sold on, as with a Dutch Galliot in 1856 and the schooner *Conductor* in 1872. In 1862, the beached hull of the *Coleen Bawn* was auctioned off 'as it lies' (on the Bull) with anchors, chains, rigging and sails. In 1868, the *Cockaleekie* – copper fastened to the bottom and partially sheeted with zinc – was similarly disposed of as a 'wreck sale' at an auction in Crosby's stores in the city (details could be obtained from John Walsh, an agent for insurers Lloyds). Sometimes the sale was cargo; in 1875, for example, slates from the *Aeron Bell* were auctioned.

Reuse was common when cargo itself washed ashore. Then, irrespective of the law, it was a case of finders keepers. In 1908, bales of soft goods, boxes of soap, spars and planks, and a baby's bassinette (cradle) were thrown up by the sea. No one seems to have known what vessel they might have come from, but carts quickly appeared and appropriated them. Coal, which was heavily imported into Dublin, also appears to have been a commonly found and taken object. As late as the twentieth century, a group of men known as long shore men made a haggard living through selling their finds. Humans were not the only beneficiaries. Towards the end of 1925, when a corn ship, the *Hamburg* (not to be confused with the *Hampton*), was driven on the shore of the Bull, greenfinches, linnets, chaffinches, house sparrows and the infrequent brambling flocked to the shore; to save the ship its cargo had been thrown overboard.

Accompanying the treasures of the sea, we regularly find accounts of items of value lost on the island. These were detailed in Dublin's *Lost and Found* columns, and included a gold watch with a monogram on the back; a lost red leather purse containing three sovereigns and keys; a silver matchbox; a Newfoundland dog; and, somewhat uniquely, a brown mare. However not everything found was actually lost. In 1908, Patrick Hogan was charged with illegally possessing a lady's gold keyless watch. Hogan stated that he had found the watch on the Bull Wall. This does not seem to have been disputed, but had the prisoner found it in a certain lady's pocket at the time? Clearer was the case in 1904, when 'sand carters' Patrick Mulvey and Patrick Mulroy were prosecuted for trespass and assault, while attempting to remove sand. Ditto in 1910, when one Michael Byrne was prosecuted for trying to remove shingle near the wall. Nearby in the dunes, *Philonicus albiceps* – the dune robber fly – passes unnoticed, lying in wait for insects flying overhead.

But life's most valuable things have no monetary value. In 1902, Michael Curley found the body of a boy enclosed in a deal box, in the sand 'near the Bull'. On a Sunday morning the previous year, William Kelly found the body of a one-week-old infant 400 yards from the coast guard station. What happened in both cases is unknown. All that can be salvaged from this era of high child mortality is the reminder that it continues elsewhere today.

Lost and Found – Notes

On jailed tenants (Brady, K., 2008, p. 228); strictly speaking, we could go back to 1641 to find mention of plundering of a barque, but the supposed events occurred in a charged political atmosphere (see earlier notes for 'A Long Finger').

On inhuman villains (Anon., 1756, *Belfast Newsletter*, p. 2).

On Sheridan (Brady, K., 2008, p. 231); Richard Nevil was awarded the freedom of the city in 1776 for procuring an act to prevent the plundering of shipwrecks (De Courcy, 1996).

On the *Premier* (Anon., 1855, May 26, *Freeman's Journal*, p. 4) which is near the spot where the barque *The Scotland* was lost.

On the *Lark* (Anon., 1757, March 29, *Belfast Newsletter*, p. 2).

On the *Speculation* (Anon., 1787, September 20, *Freeman's Journal*, p. 4.)

On the battery (Brady, K., 2008, p. 231).

The people of Clontarf 'were noted smugglers' cites McIntyre from what appears to be an early eighteenth century text (McIntyre, 1987).

On Jamaican vessel (Anon., 1790, August 18, *Finns Leinster Journal*, p. 1).

On a Dutch Galliot (Anon., 1856, November 7, *Freeman's Journal*, p. 3).

On the *Conductor* (Anon., 1872, 'Mercantile sales', *Freeman's Journal*, p. 8).

On the *Coleen Bawn* (Anon., 1862, March 25, 'Wreck Sale', *Belfast Newsletter*, p. 2).

On the *Cockaleekie* (Anon., 1868, August 8, 'Wreck Sale', *The Irish Times).*

In 1788, we find that the London brig *Lively*, which struck the Bull in a SSE gale (laden with tea and sugar and hops) was insurable for up to £2,800 (Anon., 1788, January 4, *Belfast Newsletter*, p. 2).

On *Aeron Bell* (Anon., 1875, June 18, 'Mercantile Sales', *Freeman's Journal*, p. 8).

On bassinette etc. (Anon., 1908, 'Wreckage at Dollymount', *The Irish Times*, p. 6). *The Freeman's Journal* adds shirts, hosiery and ladies underwear to the list (Anon., 1908, October 28, 'Wreckage at the Bull', *Freeman's Journal*, p. 5; Brady, K., 2008).

Speaking of coal, coal fish (*P.Virens*), also known as black pollock, were also observed in 1977 (Jeffrey, 1977).

On long shore men (Knowles, 1970). Knowles also states that a dead baby was once washed up at Clontarf, that dead dogs were plentiful in January when dog licences were due, and that barrels of paraffin oil or Guinness, wine or spirits were also common. The latter automatically became the property of the receiver of the wrecks; long shore men often traded their finds (McIntyre, 1987). The earliest record of a scavenger in the city dates to 1632 and appears to have been one Catherine Stronge alias White (Flood, D.T., 1975, *Dublin Historical Record*, Vol. 28, No. 4 , pp. 142-153).

On items lost on the island (Anon., 1906, July 20, 'Lost and Found' *The Irish Times*; Anon., 1893, August 30, 'Lost and Found' *The Irish Times*, p. 2; Anon., 1889, April 24, 'Lost',

Freeman's Journal, p. 1; Anon., 1898, July 5, *Freeman's Journal*, p. 1; Anon., 1875, October 23, 'Found', *Freeman's Journal*, p. 23).

On Hogan (Anon., 1908, Septewmber 1, 'Police Courts', *The Irish Times*, p. 3).

Not that an owner of lost property was necessary for prosecution: Robert Gaven and Michael Monaghan were charged with attempting to pawn a pearl and gold scarf pin, with horseshoe and whip entwined. They claimed that they had found it on the North Bull Wall; even though there was no apparent owner, they were charged anyway (Anon., 1908, June 29, 'Owner of a pin wanted', *Freeman's Journal*, p. 7).

On sand carters (Anon., 1904, November 22, *Freeman's Journal*, p. 6).

Removing shingle was contrary to the board of trade regulations (Anon., 1910, September 5, 'Raheny Petty Sessions', *The Irish Times*).

On the boy in the box (Anon., 1902, August 11, 'A Child's Body Found', *Freeman's Journal*, p. 12).

On the infant (Anon., 1901, July 16, 'Gruesome discovery at the North Bull', *Freeman's Journal*, p. 9).

31

The Bird Girl

In the collective memory of literary Dubliners, a girl stands in the water of Bull Island. She is known as the bird girl. The girl's fame is secured because her image is burned into the soul of Stephen Dedalus – the self-portrait of Dublin's most famous scribbler, James Joyce:

> A girl stood before him in midstream, alone and still, gazing out to sea. She seemed like one whom magic had changed into the likeness of a strange and beautiful seabird. Her long slender bare legs were delicate as a crane's and pure save where an emerald trail of seaweed had fashioned itself as a sign upon the flesh. Her thighs, fuller and soft-hued as ivory, were bared almost to the hips, where the white fringes of her drawers were like feathering of soft white down. Her slate-blue skirts were kilted boldly about her waist and dovetailed behind her. Her bosom was as a bird's, soft and slight, slight and soft as the breast of some dark-plumaged dove. But her long fair hair was girlish: and girlish, and touched with the wonder of mortal beauty, her face.

For early twentieth century Ireland, this is carnal stuff. The scene, which in that typical Joycean manner appears seminal in both a literal and figurative sense, makes academics quiver and tremble even more than its characters (her appearance occurs immediately after Dedalus has decided to create 'a living thing, new and soaring and beautiful, impalpable, imperishable'; a flame trembles in her face when she spies him, causing a profane joy in Dedalus). *A Portrait of the Artist* has been analysed to death. Joyce, Dedalus and the girl are hopelessly entangled in footnotes – although the passage speaks well for itself without commentary.

An earlier and quite different draft that forms some of the material of *A Portrait of the Artist* was called *Stephen Hero*. In that version, we are told that Stephen spent the great part of his summer on the rocks of the North Bull (at one time Joyce lived just down the road at 8 Inverness Road in Fairview). The bird girl – in so much as she can be identified – is called Lucy (Joyce may have named his daughter Lucia in her memory). But actual details of her presence on the island and the island itself – if they were ever written – have not survived. Joyce threw the rejected manuscript in the fire (lingering bitterness of the rejection can later be found in Joyce's 1912 poetical tirade against printers and publishers, 'Gas from a Burner', where, among other things, Curley's Hole also gets a brief mention: It's a wonder to me, upon my soul, / he forgot to mention Curly's Hole).

By *Finnegans Wake*, a dance of words in which Lucia's life features significantly, the island itself is submerged in a labyrinth of wordplay, with only the odd obvious surfacing of its presence: 'the first grey streaks steal silvering by for to mock their quarrels in dollymount tumbling'. And in this shipwreck of clues there may well be a stronger connection between Joyce's writing and Bull Island than hitherto thought. In the earlier and more accessible *Ulysses*, though, the island's fate lies under dark clouds indeed. At Dollymount, Leopold Bloom (aka Odysseus) now muses on a scheme to enclose the peninsular delta of the North Bull and erect on the space of the foreland, used for golf links and rifle ranges, an asphalted esplanade with casinos, booths, shooting galleries, hotels, boarding houses, reading rooms and establishments for mixed bathing. The bird girl finds resonance in a sad and downcast Gerty. And across the bay at nearby Sandymount, Stephen's meditation by the sea encounters 'a porterbottle stood up, stogged to its waist', the 'bloated carcass of a dog lay lolled on bladderwrack' and the sandflats 'waited to suck his treading soles, breathing upward sewage breath'. This urban dystopia contrasts starkly with an earlier writing where Joyce's imagination seemed more in joyful harmony with Bull Island: to a sea-harvest of shells, sand nooks, sandknolls; to arid grasses and brackish water; to seawrack, foreshore, and breakwater.

Though Joyce himself was a noted schemer of all sorts of Walter Mitty-like projects, Bloom's particular vision of the island's destruction is not fanciful. In fact, it reflects the everyman thinking of early twentieth century Dublin with some accuracy – except perhaps for the ultimate bookworm's fantasy: reading rooms.

The Bird Girl – Notes

Mrs Joyce saved what she could from the fire.

A parody of a Bull Island passage is also present in *Finnegans*

Wake (Carver, C., 1978, 'James Joyce and the theory of magic', *James Joyce Quarterly*, 15(3), 201-214).

It is worth mentioning in passing that it is well known that Joyce subscribed to Victor Bérards 1902 account of the Phoenician origin of the Odyssey (*Les Phéniciens et l'Odyssée*). And at the end of the eighteenth century Charles Vallency had claimed in a series of works, which were familiar to Joyce, that the original Irish settlers were Phoenician. Interestingly, in 1810, this popular origin myth was noted by William Cusack-Smith in his book *The Anonymous*. We don't know if Joyce read *The Anonymous* but we do know that Tyre was an ancient Phoenician city, and that Cusack-Smith claimed that the city of 'Dubullin' was founded after a Tyrian vessel struck on the North Bull. The reference to Bull Island, Phoenicians and Ulysses all in the same tract may have lurked in Joyce's imagination (Cusack-Smith, William, 1810, *The Anonymous*, London, J. McCreery).

A scheme like Bloom's did exist in Dublin – although seemingly without Joyce's fantasy of reading rooms.

32

The Blue Lagoon

To contextualise Bloom's musings we need to understand that, as far back as 1900, the *Freeman's Journal* could note that the North Bull was one of the prettiest and most pleasant places in Dublin. Even in its dishevelled and neglected condition, its possibilities were deemed illimitable – as bathing place, a bicycle track, or fashionable promenade. Bloom's fantasy, commonly voiced, is best understood as a gasping counterpoint to the city's slums, decay and unemployment. The dreaming took various forms. In 1921, for example, J. Ryan proposed building a dam on this 'long finger-shaped island' and with the aid of strong ebb and flow to generate electric power (at the wall). But, as with Bloom's contribution, this and other such schemes lived as much in the mind as in actuality. Of them all, however, the so-called 'Blue Lagoon' project was the one that was taken most seriously.

By 1929, a Dublin Corporation committee was being assembled to consider a scheme first mooted by one Hudson some 30 years earlier: to build in the first instance a 'marine lake' from Sutton to Dollymount, and in doing so, to create a three-mile-long motor boat racing circuit. This would necessitate a road from the mainland to the island and a dam crossing from Sutton to the north tip of the island.

Opposition to the scheme was immediately voiced. In 1929, Rev. P.G. Kennedy gave a Photography Salon Lecture on 'Bird Watching on the North Bull' using lantern slides. In between discussing goosander, the rare smew, and various 'globe spanners', Kennedy is recorded as arguing that any attempt to construct a Blue Lagoon would lead to increased costs for dredging the harbour.

Doubtless Kennedy said even more. Nevertheless, the proponents of development steadily advanced their cause. In 1931, the secretary of the Metropolitan Marine Lake Conference would argue that creating a municipal aerodrome and pleasure resort would show thousands of visitors that 'Dublin is a really progressive city'. Being the 1930s, such 'progressive' ideas were promoted by proto-fascist torchlight processions to Dollymount, flights from the strand, fictitious 'bombing' of speed boats, naval battles, burning oil wells, bonfires and aquatic fireworks.

In 1936, ornithologist Thomas H. Mason wrote a letter to *The Irish Times* arguing against the Blue Lagoon project and its dubious arguments of national pride and employment. It would be a crime, argued Mason, that a beautiful place should be desecrated by the vulgarity of the showman and the noises of the sea boat. The destruction of the amenities should not be tolerated. Like Kennedy, Mason argued that any interference with the tides around the Bull might have disastrous consequences, not just for the Bull, but for the port of Dublin itself. But, of coure, the chief concern of both men was the birds of the island.

With the advent of war, all public talk of the project disappeared. But by 1944 Kennedy was again warning of the threat of a possible people's pleasure ground, which he described as a sort of 'Coney Island'. Kennedy's protests went ignored, but planning was indeed being carried out in secret. The Dublin Naturalists Field Club and the Irish Society for the Protection of Birds had been refused access to information by the Minister for Industry and Commerce and his unlikely accessory to the scheme, the Irish Tourist Board. And by 1946, provisional approval was granted to build a recreation and amusement centre, which were part of the Blue Lagoon scheme.

The proposal quickly stalled when engineers weighed in against the project. The exact reasons are unclear but it was most likely due to fears that damage might be inflicted on the harbour. (If engineers needed any reminding of the importance of keeping the port sand-free, they got it later in December 1950 when the auxiliary schooner *The Antelope* ran aground on the sands near Dollymount in heavy gales.) As such, the grandiose design of a Blue Lagoon from Sutton to Fairview was suspended by 1946. A subsequently downsized lake scheme along the back of the Bull to the Black Banks near Sutton also collapsed because it emerged that the smaller lake would have been unsuitable for seaplanes and high speed boating.

This left only a modest, but still destructive, scheme for the island itself. This would involve an embankment from Watermill Lane to the island by a causeway that threatened to silt up the saltmarshes. It would also include the provision of a restaurant, dance hall, an open air theatre, amusement park and various other amenities, plus a road along the north of the island for traffic to inaccessible parts of the island (this road might have left the island via a bridge to Sutton). As the plan was still destructive, Mason continued his protests in 1949, arguing that turning a large part of the island into a fun-fair was vandalism. And that the project involved removing a beautiful old bridge in a famous beauty spot and replacing it with a concrete structure so that motorists could speed to their death.

By 1949, it seems that the protests, combined with the fact that the Blue Lagoon project had to a large extent already been economically disembowelled, meant that even this last rem-nant of the project was being tacitly shelved. Reclaiming the shore from Dollymount to Howth was also considered prob-lematic because of a lack of filling material. It was deemed unlikely that any progress would be possible 'for some time'. Instead, scientific assessment of the marine growth at the 'marine lake' was in progress.

The island's ornithologists nevertheless remained vigilant. In 1950, Miss A. M. Wigham of the Irish Society for the Protec-tion of Birds continued to stress that building an amusement park would be disastrous and that attempts to lease the land to a cross channel company were disturbing (with memories of earlier Irish trade wars with Britain still fresh, this was a strong card). Similarly, in 1953 *The Irish Times* remarked that it would be a pity if a valuable 'lung' should be sacrificed for a new Coney Island. By 1954, more complaints could be found in the *Southern Star*. But by now the initial Blue Lagoon scheme had definitely been more or less abandoned, even if plans for a road along the inside channel to Howth continued to lurk on some engineer's desk.

From inception to close, the threat of major development on the island had lasted nearly half a century – that is, if it has gone away.

The Blue Lagoon – Notes

On dishevelled condition (Anon., 1900, April 10, *Freeman's Journal*, p. 9).

Even earlier, in 1843, John Gresham had failed to construct a pleasure ground on the sea front as agreed in a lease given by Vernon. Although Vernon seems to have kept a commitment he made not to plant trees on the North Bull (in order not to block Gresham's view).

On Ryan's scheme (Anon., 1921, June 29, *Freeman's Journal*, p. 3).

Other plans by the Dollymount Improvement Committee to toll visitors (to hear a band) were also being formulated around 1905 (Anon., 1905, March 10, 'The Bull Wall', *Irish Independent*, p. 4).

On Sutton dam (Anon., 1932, July 6, 'Marine Lake', *The Irish Times*).

Kennedy on dredging (Anon., 1929, September 12, 'Photography Salon Lecture', *The Irish Times*).

A progressive city (Anon., 1930, January 8, *Irish Independent*, p. 8).

On torchlight processions (Anon., 1932, May 11, 'Irish Birds never better protected', *Irish Independent*, p. 7).

Mason was horrified when he first heard of the project, and breathed a sigh of relief when he thought it was dead. But then in 1936 it was revived again (Mason, T.H., 1936, August 12, 'Letter to the Editor', *The Irish Times*).

On Coney Island (Anon., 1944, September 22, 'Bird life in the west is different', *The Irish Times*, p. 3).

On Tourist Board (Anon., 1946, June 7, 'Ireland may have a national trust', *The Irish Times*, p. 3).

In all likelihood the amusement centre component of the scheme was more of a sweetener to the public. The economic value lay in the construction of the lagoon and any commercial activities that could be operated within it. If that project failed, so would 'Coney Island'.

On engineers objecting (Anon., 1946, November 6, '97,000 Lake Scheme at Dollymount', *The Irish Times*, p. 3).

The *Antelope* couldn't be got off and was eventually demolished, in part with explosives (Lowth, F.C., 2002, 'Shipwrecks around Dublin Bay', *Dublin Historical Record*, 55(1), 50-63).

In 1910, people had waited at dawn (in vain) for the coming of cross channel aviators – or 'heavenly fliers' – in the hope that they might land at Dollymount or indeed Sandymount (Anon., 1910, August 20, 'The Coming Aviators', *The Irish Times*, p. 23).

The city was advised by engineer Sir Claud Inglis and Bayler Butler, a biological advisor (Anon., 1946, November 16, 'Corporation plan recreational centre in the city', *The Irish Times*, p. 15). It was thought that the water may have clotted with algae (personal conversation with Tom Cooney).

On an open air theatre etc. (Anon., 1946, November 16, 'Corporation Plan recreational centre in the city', *The Irish Times*, p. 15). The plan involved the development of 86 acres at the Bull Wall.

On a bridge to Sutton (Farrington, A. and Haughton, J.P., 1947, April, 'The North Bull Island', *The Irish Naturalists Journal*, 9(2), 46-48).

Mason's objections (Anon., 1949, March 22, 'Vandalism in Ireland', *The Irish Times*, p. 5).

Perhaps further complicating matters for the city was the fact that the socially powerful Royal Dublin Golf Club already occupied significant parts of the land they envisaged developing. And though weakened by a loss of a clubhouse it probably didn't share the council vision of the great unwashed turning up on its borders.

On scientific assessment (Anon., 1949, July 5, 'Amusement plan for blue lagoon', *The Irish Times*).

Wigham's objections (Anon., 1950, May 6, 'Amusement Park Protest', *The Irish Times*).

A valuable lung (Anon., 1953, November 24, 'An Irishman's Diary, *The Irish Times*, p. 5).

On road plans (Anon., 1953, November 2, 'Ireland's first bird sanctuary threatened?' *The Irish Times*).

Later revisionists would claim that the lagoon plan had been literally and symbolically destroyed by the dumping of rubbish on the island (Anon., 1972, March 16, 'Clean Living', *Irish Press*, p. 10).

33

The Causeway

The one thing that did get built in the 1960s – despite all
protests – was the causeway. In order to accommodate
more cars and further development plans, this unedifying
roadway was built across 'the whip of the waters', where the
two ecologically crucial scouring tides around the island met.
As predicted, it immediately caused rapid sedimentation of
the western side of the causeway, immediately dooming the
mussel there to extinction. By 1970, Kilbarrack Sailing Club
also complained that even Sutton Creek was silting up and
that pollution was increasing since the causeway was built.
In spite of that, or indeed because of it, the rods used to mea-
sure the silting up were replaced in 1986 in favour of ones that
measured a growing environmental threat: radioactivity from
Sellafield in England.

Sean Dublin Bay Loftus also maintained that the causeway exacerbated flooding. More readily observable, however,
was a notable shift in traffic behaviour. Traffic increased to
parts of the island that were hitherto left alone by most car
owners. Increasingly, cars could drive on to the sands, laden
with bathers and rubbish, followed by food traders with yet

more rubbish. In 1978, this caused environmentalists to plead that cars and motorbikes be at least excluded from conservation zones. But two years later, the Corporation appeared to be tolerant of even grossly destructive activities such as motorcycle scrambling in the dunes. With the beach being used as a car park and unmarked roadway, it also became a learner driver location where various tragedies naturally ensued, the most notable being the death of a two-year-old infant in 1982 – knocked down by a driver observing the 12 miles per hour speed limit introduced in 1965 to protect children. For the poet Kevin Faller, the causeway's damage to the island was perceived as fatal to the island as well. In 'Lament for Bull Island' he mourned 'a thousand lovers could not save you'.

The corporation was immensely proud of the new road. When it sponsored Dorothy Forde's popular glossy photo-catalogue of *The Wild Flowers of North Bull Island*, a photograph of the causeway's roundabout graces the book's cover – not a flower in sight. Adjacent to the roundabout, one can see the interpretive centre that was built in 1986. It is everything a badly designed building should be and so immensely ugly that it calls to be knocked down (an opinion shared by staff). Inside – if you can find it open or get up the stairs – you can be disappointed by a stuffed short eared owl, a peregrine, and one or two other bits of dusty clutter. In this European-funded ornithology and environment centre, a wildlife film on the Bull by one or Ireland's great conservationists, Éamon de Buitléar, is no longer on display.

The Causeway – Notes

It is possible that at least one serious attempt to blow up the causeway was considered by protesters. In 1972, the army were called to remove sticks of gelignite from its verges. The gelignite had first been discovered by two boys, Noel (14) and Anthony (11) McDonald. The army had been alerted after Mrs McDonald found part of the stash under their beds. Equally, it may have been an IRA arms dump.

Dawson states the 'whip of the water' was where the James Larkin and Howth Roads met. Local men called it the desert on account of its desolate nature (Dawson, T., 1976, 'The road to Howth', *Dublin Historical Record*, 29(4), pp. 122-132).

In 1937, one Mr. Mallagh, an engineer, had opposed the causeway scheme on the grounds that this scouring water would cause considerable risk to the navigable channel (Anon., 1937, April 23, *Irish Press*, p. 9).

In 'Lament for Bull Island', Faller notes that rubble from the burned mansion of St Anne's was dumped in the lagoon to 'make a parking lot of Dollymount Strand' (Faller, Kevin, 1973, *Lament for the Bull Island*, Dublin, Goldsmith Press).

On silting (Anon., 1970, February 19, *Irish Press*, p. 14).

The silting was described as rapid (Healy, Brenda, 1975, 'Fauna of the Salt-Marsh, North Bull Island, Dublin', *Proceedings of the Royal Irish Academy*, 75, 225-244).

On rods (Anon., 1986, March 13,. *Irish Press*, p. 4).

On Loftus (McIntyre, 1987).

Increasing car numbers were exacerbated by the causeway. 'I could count the number of cars at Dollymount in 1939 with a glance, not so today said a regular visitor' (Anon., 1960, January 23, *Irish Press*, p. 1).

On cars (Anon., 1966, June 7, *Irish Press*, p. 4).

On car exclusion zones (Anon., 1978, January 20, *Irish Press*, p. 6).

On motorbikes (Anon., 1980, April 2, 'An island scramble', *Irish Press*, p. 8).

On speed limit (Anon., 1965, January 20, 'Experts to work on cleaner Liffey', *Irish Press*, p. 4).

On infant's death (Anon., 1982, July 24, *Irish Press*, p. 8). A proposal by Deputy Ned Brennan that the driving of cars should be banned on Dublin beaches came to nothing on Bull Island; Knowles's memoir states that with the growing presence of motor cars the island began to lose its charm (Knowles, 1970).

Faller also wrote a poem titled 'Bull Wall Sunset' (Faller, 1973). Elsewhere, Austin Clarke's 1950's 'Flock at Dawn' briefly alludes to a tumble at Dollymount. The list of writers and poets who have referenced the Bull is legion.

In 1978, 2,500 plus ecology students were thought to be visiting the island (Anon., 1978, January 20, *Irish Press*, p. 6).

The interpretive centre was built in 1986 with EEC funding, supposedly as 'an ornithology and environment centre'. On the upside, an Éamon de Buitléar wildlife film was on display and the views are quite good (Anon., 1984, May 1, *Irish Press*, p. 16). De Buitléar's series *World of Wildlife* also featured Bull Island (Anon., 1977, April 15, *Irish Press*, p. 15).

34

Mice, Fleas, Foxes, Hares

Two pairs of foxes now live on the island. It is not known when foxes first came to the island, although we do know they were definitely there in 1890, either as natives or 'imported'. We know this because a local association, the Clontarf Beagles met in early January to hunt one. Possibly they migrated with blue hare and rabbits across the mudflats at low tide.

By 1931, Eugene O Mahony had noted that the rabbits had noticeably declined in population due to ferreting. (Not all attempts to hunt rabbits were successful. When two cousins, Paul Gilmore and James Doherty, went digging for rabbits in the dunes in 1955, two tonnes of sand swallowed them. Rescuers digging with bare hands found them after 15 minutes – they had initially dug in the wrong place – but only Gilmore survived). The rabbits further suffered from outbreaks of *myxomatosis*, which unintentionally collapsed European rabbit populations after the *myxoma virus* was experimentally introduced to Europe in the 1950s by French bacteriologist Paul Felix Armand-Delille. The virus arrived on the Bull sometime after 1953. Swelling of the eyes, skin tumours, blindness and death followed swiftly. Hares were also susceptible.

The island's blue hare is so called because in theory they can turn a bluish grey in winter, although Bull Island hares tend to simply become duller and less russet. It may be a more recent arrival on the island. In 1930, a Mr. Jerry Connolly appears to have released two hares on to St Anne's golf links. Five years later their numbers stood in the hundreds and jokes were made that the island should be renamed 'Hare Island'. The hares were viewed as harmless to the golf course, and an important source of revenue. In 1934, 140 were sold to St Margaret's Coursing Club without any diminishing effect on the population. By 1937, naturalist Robert Lloyd Praeger noted that the population threatened 'to devour the island'. The hares had to be removed or captured from 'this wonderful gift from the sea'. It was illegal to kill them. Yet by 1948, they remained plentiful and illegal hare coursing at night was a regular feature on the island. (In the same year, entomologist Eugene O'Mahony produced the underappreciated work *The Fleas of the North Bull Island*; I have not read it. I have however read *The Mammal Ectoparasites of the North Bull Island, Dublin Bay*. In this work, O'Mahony describes how they were found gorging on a warm dead rabbit, a dead rat and a dead Guillemot.)

In 1955, six hares were spotted sitting in their shallow 'forms', which they had scrapped out in the mudflats at low tide. Perhaps because of this all too visible presence, the netting of hares was made legal on the island in 1958 (though it was quickly objected to). At some point, their numbers were restocked and managed by Dublin and District Coursing Club, until a ban on netting them in 1961. The club claimed that the ban would result in disease from inbreeding, which would be far more dangerous to the existing hare population than netting some of them. As a result of this argument, which cleverly resonated with concerns over rabbit deaths, the ban was partially lifted. Hares could be netted every two years.

The Society of Prevention of Cruelty to Animals, the golf clubs, the Bull Island Amenities Association (BIAA) and the Irish Society for the Protection of Wild Birds (ISPWB) all opposed the practice of netting. But greyhound trainers, supported by influential TD's such as Fianna Fáil's Noel Lemass (son of Taoiseach Sean Lemass), continued to argue that interbreeding had increasingly left the hare population weak and prone to disease; if they were not thinned out they would be wiped out.

The BIAA countered that only one in nine hares actually appeared to have died from disease, but these had in fact been the victim of dogs. In any case, other breeding stock could be introduced to prevent any fatal interbreeding. In 1964, the conservationists estimated the numbers to be below 100 (the club intended to catch up to 50).

With opportunistic and casual political support for netting, the hares appear to have become progressively rarer. Yet somehow the hares continued to survive, possibly by taking advantage of shelter on the golf courses. By 1973, the hares that remained on St Anne's grounds were reported as tame – with a few well-nourished hawks living nearby. In 1978, members of the Dublin Coursing Club were finally convicted of illegally netting hares on the island.

By 1986, hares were plentiful enough to herd them over to St Anne's Park during a golf championship and back again at 4.00 am in the morning for a number of days running. But then numbers dropped alarmingly: only 25 existed in 1994. In 1995, an attempt to boost numbers was made with 28 wild hares being introduced from Mosney. But this was ineffective.

In the following years, dogs, rifles, shotguns, crossbows, long bows and sling shots were all used to hunt them illegally. In 2013, only a handful of these nocturnal creatures were spotted by ecologists. Not enough, it seems, to breed successfully.

In 1895, Dr. H. Lyster Jameson found a colony of mice inhabiting the sand hills. These were an isolated colony of the common house mouse – *Mus Musclus jamesoni Krausse*. The mice gained international fame after mouseologists and Darwinists demonstrated that their pale sandy colour had evolved over a very short number of years. This colour helped the mice hide from hawks. Alas, the very fame of the poor mice ensured that some thirty-six of them ended up in the national museum – stuffed. But some were still recorded as present in the dunes and cottages in 1931. By 1971, the house mouse was reported to be interbreeding with the field mouse along the Bull Wall – and the very legitimacy of Jameson's mouse was being called into question.

By then, the unusually bold brown rat and Ireland's smallest mammal the pigmy shrew – which looks very much like a conical cartoon mouse – were also present on the island. Curiously – because of a high metabolic rate – the pygmy shrew will starve to death if it doesn't eat every four hours.

Mice, Fleas, Foxes, Hares – Notes

Anon., 1890, January 4, 'Clontarf Beagles', *The Irish Times*, p. 6.

The blue hare, *Lepus timidus hibernicus* (Jeffrey, 1977, p. 112). Moffat thought that hares were capable of swimming across to the island (Moffat, C.B., 1937, 'The mammals of Ireland', *Proceedings of the Royal Irish Academy. Section B: Biological, Geological, and Chemical Science*, 44, pp. 61-128).

At some unspecified time point, rabbits used to be common along the breakwater and an area known as 'Lady Anne Bank' (Jeffrey, 1977, p. 112).

On ferretting (Jeffrey, 1977, p. 112). Mahony lived in Dollymount and once reported capturing a gold tailed moth at his study lamp (Mahony, E., 1934, 'An Irish Record for Goldtail Moth', *Irish Naturalists' Journal*, 5(5), 121).

On dead boys (Anon., 1955, September 3, 'Two ton fall', *Southern Star*, p. 1).

On Hare Island (McIntyre, 1987).

On St Margaret's Coursing Club (Anon., 1935, January 9, 'Hares that like to see golfers', *Irish Independent*, p. 9).

Praeger, R. L. (1937). *The way that I went*, Dublin, Hodges Figgis.

On illegal coursing (Anon., 1948, July 24, *Irish Independent*, p. 4.)

O'Mahony, Eugene, 1947, 'The mammal ectoparasites of the North Bull Island, Dublin Bay', *Irish Naturalists' Journal*, 9(3), 78-79).

On shallow forms (Moriatry, C., 1955, July, 'Behaviour of hares on mud flats', *The Irish Naturalists Journal*, 11(11), 310).

On legal netting (Anon., 1958, October 23, *Irish Press*, p. 6).

Anon., 1961, March 9, 'Hare ban hits club', *Irish Press*, p. 17.

Anon., 1964, January 13, 'SPCA to fight netting permit', *Irish Press*, p. 3.

On preventing interbreeding (Anon., 1964, January 15, *Irish Press*, p. 10).

On low hare numbers (Anon., 1964, January 21, *Irish Press*, p. 9).

In 1966, it was also claimed that the hare had been hunted by dogs (Anon., 1966, February 1, *Irish Press*, p. 9).

On hawks (Anon., 1973, September 27, 'Golf can be hare raising', *Irish Press*, p. 3).

On conviction (Anon., 1978, March 29, 'The selling of hares', *Irish Press*, p. 8).

On championship (Anon., 1984, August 3, *Irish Press*, p. 1).

Some hare were tracked with radio collars; the hare was described as fundamentally nocturnal, spending much of their time resting or feeding (Wolfe, A., Long, A. M. and Corrigan, P., 2002, 'Behaviour of Irish mountain hares on coastal grassland', *The Irish Naturalists' Journal*, 27(2), 57-65).

On evolution of the mouse (Jeffrey, 1977).

The museum now displays two Dollymount house mice from 1901.

The British Museum thought the samples sent to it resembled the Steppe Mouse (Mahony, E., 1937, 'On some forms of the house mouse, Mus musculus Linn, in Ireland,' *Irish Naturalists' Journal*, 6(12), 288-290).

For more on mouse interbreeding see O'Gorman in Jeffrey (1977). Also, it has been argued that the mouse may have been an Egyptian stowaway (Anon., 1990, January 22, *Irish Press*, p. 21). The idea of an Egyptian mouse may have stemmed from comments by Moffat (Moffat, C.B., 1937, 'The mammals of Ireland', *Proceedings of the Royal Irish Academy. Section B: Biological, Geological, and Chemical Science*, 44, pp. 61-128).

35

Fire and the Alder Marsh

Around May 1885, the Dublin Golf Club was founded on Grafton Street as a result of the initiative of banker John Lumsden. The third such club in Ireland, it had moved from Phoenix Park to Sutton and then finally to Bull Island around 1889. At this stage, it was a golf links in the most authentic sense of the term. Land could pretty much only be manipulated manually. Pesticides were seldom used (though artificial manure did exist). And grazing animals would have been relied upon for cropping vegetation. For all that, as far back as 1889, golf on the island was being cryptically referenced by *The Irish Times* as an implement of destruction.

Despite being subject to merciless ridicule, 250 members paid a £2 membership fee with an 8 guineas entrance fee – well beyond the reaches of the common Dubliner. The club further received the designation 'Royal' in 1891. The grounds stretched over a considerable portion of the island, which was then substantially smaller than it is today. Public rights to the land were restricted. In 1903, three men were prosecuted for removing sand from the golf 'banks' (although they claimed they were entitled to do so, because they had the necessary permits from the Vernons).

Hints of growing social tension between golf club members and less privileged users of the island occur in the same decade. In 1909, bathers observed that their rights to bathing facilities – which affected thousands – were being blocked by the Port and Docks Board. Some of the board's members – complained the bathers – were also members of Royal Dublin. In the same period the Port and Docks Board had also continuously refused a modest request by the Dublin United Trades and Labour Institute to erect a temporary marquee tent on the Bull sands. Yet these particular tensions came to a rapid halt, for two particular reasons. First, the bathers got their shelters by agitating with 'outdoor parliaments', and second, the Great War intervened.

To be exact, while players such as the famous Birdie Moran found themselves fatally entangled in the horrors of battle at Le Cateau, France, the British military commandeered the island, banned bathing, and blew the Royal Dublin fairways to pieces with artillery and rifle practice. The odd shell and bullet still crops up. Any lingering social tensions seem to have dissipated with the defeat of Larkin and the unions in the Dublin Lockout, and the upheaval caused by the Irish War of Independence and Irish Civil War (which, of course, was anything but civil).

With the war at an end, Royal Dublin received compensation and reconstructed its course. A second club, St Anne's Golf Club, was also formed in 1921, with only nine holes. Both clubs' initial interactions with the island's wildlife appears to have been fairly considerate. In 1926, a groundsman at St Anne's fixed a stake to the ground near a nest 20 yards in fror of the putting ground, and with the consideration of golfers, a ringed plover successfully hatched her brood. In 1931, the caddie master of the Royal similarly used to regularly feed the starlings (and a year earlier, golfers had rescued a skylark from a peregrine). Linnets also used to breed in the clubhouse gardens and other nests were tolerated on clubhouse property. As with the Royal, members of St Anne's quickly developed an interest in ornithology, and even before the island was made a sanctuary golfers warned off bird catchers. When the island was made a sanctuary in 1931 they supported the move. And for reasons such as these, birdwatcher Kennedy spoke highly of the clubs' interactions with wildlife.

All this time, however, the futures of both clubs lay under a growing cloud. Despite the social power of many of the clubs members, the various Blue Lagoon schemes suggested moving or sweeping them away entirely. Strictly speaking, St Anne's future was slightly more uncertain. As second comer, it did not have first say in any shuffling of locations that might result from the various plans under development. It was hoping for the best, but preparing for the worst. However, problems were exacerbated for the Royal when, by chance, their 39-year-old 'Norwegian' clubhouse caught fire in 1943. Flames lit up the night sky and could be seen from the city. Thanks to the cries of a cat, 14 people were saved in the middle of the night – but not the building. Uncertainty caused by the Blue Lagoon plans meant the clubhouse would not be rebuilt until 1954.

To avoid possible extinction, the clubs worked together to find to an 'amicable solution': both would shuffle down the island a bit. This would have left room for some development near the wall, had the development happened (this became irrelevant when the Blue Lagoon project collapsed). Simultaneously, but in circumstances less clear, the Royal Dublin bought the entire island for £8,000, which it then sold to a suspiciously helpful corporation in 1954 for £12,000, while retaining landownership of their own 18 holes. Though legal, such a murky transaction raised eyebrows, and the shuffle itself came to be perceived not as a reaction to development proposals but as a land grab.

Class tensions once again emerged. In 1955, Frank Robbins, vice president of the Dublin Council of Trade Unions, described the actions of the golf club as 'one of the biggest pieces of robbery of democratic rights that the citizens of Dublin had ever had perpetrated on them'. Robbins claimed that the citizens were being filched of their God-given rights to enjoy the use of Bull Island, and that land had been expropriated for just 300 golfers. Protests were held and in 1956 the unions threatened a squatter's day for July the fourth. Responding to the pressure the corporation took action. It gave notice that unless St Anne's – which had claimed new territory – reverted to its pre-1947 position, it would be given notice to quit the island. Given the ultimatum, the golf club agreed. Misreading its position, the club then quickly applied for a licence for an 18-hole golf course, but this proposal was turned down.

In 1962, St Anne's Golf Club members openly expressed support for the destructive causeway, which linked to their club grounds. 'Now that we don't have to drive across the sands,' wrote one, 'we will have the satisfaction of not having to replace our car silencers each year.' And by 1964, sensing a renewed appetite for development within the corporation, they once again applied to extend their golf course. In doing so this time, the club shrewdly took officials to visit the island midweek when it seemed most lifeless (in fact the Department of Zoology in Trinity College Dublin had charted some 332 species of invertebrate fauna on the Salt Marsh alone). By October, the club secured agreement in principle to lease 40 acres from Dublin City Council. This figure of 40 acres was later discovered to be sleight of hand. The area demarcated on the map was actually some 55 acres.

The Bull Island Amenities Association immediately objected: the interests of a mere 200 golfers were now outweighing the leisure interests of 500,000; it was the people's property, enough had been reserved for golfers. The original sale of the island by the Vernon Estate to Lord Ardilaun stipulated that the public continued to enjoy the rights to walk over the lands and bathe from the foreshore. The national trust, An Taisce, also objected to the plan, as did groups such as the St Anne's Resident Association, under the motto 'the most good for the most people'. For some, Bull Island was a gift from God. The city manager was deluged by letters from people all over Dublin. In 1965, an already under pressure city corporation decided to make no decision until after the causeway was fully completed.

Despite the public outcry, an astonishing speech by Dublin's Fianna Fáil Lord Mayor in 1967 urged the golf club to 'fight all the way'. St Anne's seems – quite correctly – to have taken this as an indicator of political sanctuary from on high, and as a licence to ignore local authorities. In 1973, a road built to their club house without proper planning permission was described by Dublin City Council as 'illegal and a serious breach of planning permission'. The validity of planning permission for the club house was further called into question. Yet official city council letters were ignored by the club. In an oral hearing, other objections regarding the club followed from An Taisce and a collective known as the Living City Group. Yet in spite of all this, in 1975 the club managed to secure final permission for their clubhouse – from the Minister for Local Government.

By 1982, the emboldened club now prepared to move further from its founders' support for nature and build on the ecologically important Alder marsh. The club further refused to wait on decisions on impact assessment by the 'General Purposes Committee of Dublin Corporation' before they would expand their golf course. In doing so it was well aware that birds nested in the marsh and that numerous important species grew there and indeed were protected under wildlife acts (for example, rare wild asparagus).

But political sanctuary does not necessarily guarantee social sanctuary. On 9 April 1982, St Anne's was vandalised. Four greens on the nine-hole course were dug up. The inhabited clubhouse was set on fire, and the club steward and his family were lucky to escape without injury. In a letter to the editor of the *Irish Press*, Jean Norton wrote of being appalled to hear that St Anne's Golf Club was even contemplating turning its leased part of the Alder marsh into more golf links for the club. Such a rich botanical area inside a city limits was unique. Even such a peaceful letter now caused St Anne's fear; it seemed that almost anytime the club received publicity in the media it was attacked at night.

The *Irish Press* thought the dispute over the golf club might end bitterly. The decision facing the city fathers was simple: Do they stand for large numbers of people enjoying unique birds and plants in their natural habitat, or do they opt for the rights of small numbers of people to enjoy themselves playing on an artificially created area? (By 1977, both clubs had extensively modified the links from their natural state.)

For reasons unclear, the large and persuasive union protests never materialised this time around, although with heavy campaigning the environmentalists finally managed to persuade the Mayor of the merits of the Alder marsh. The corporation, seeking resolution, offered the golf club land near the saltmarsh, while the club in turn would surrender any claim to the Alder marsh and the existing club house (an alternative option for the club would involve taking possession of an old dump site – see later – but this would be more expensive). The environmentalists, then, had saved the Alder marsh (but lost other areas), while St Anne's got the land they required for their 18 holes. A story of limited resources and competing social desires finally came to an end in awkward compromise – a less bitter one than had been feared.

Visiting golfers now only hear the usual sugar sweet golf lore: around 1935, at the course at St Anne's, a raven picked up a golf ball after a drive from the first tee. It then dropped it on the fairway of the sixth hole, leaving the owner of the ball to claim the record for the longest drive in the history of golf. A godwit once entered the clubhouse of the Royal Dublin and so forth. The night in 1955, when a sweet factory owner drove on to the Royal Dublin links and killed himself with fumes from the car's exhaust pipe, is never mentioned.

Fire and the Alder Marsh – Notes

The Royal Dublin followed the earlier formation of the Royal Curragh Golf Club and the Royal Belfast.

On artificial manure (Daly, 2011).

On golf as an implement of destruction (Anon., 1889, October 31, *The Irish Times*). Not the only sport on the island of course. The Dublin rovers played the Clontarf rovers in 1882 (Anon., 1882, October 14, 'Sporting intelligence', *Freeman's Journal*, p. 7). An early mention of hurling occurs in 1908, when the John O'Mahony Hurling Club practiced on the Bull (Anon., 1908, September 29, 'Dundrum licences', *Freeman's Journal*, p.2). We also have apprentice jockeys exercising horses from as early as 1906 – 14-year-old Sam Hanley fell from his horse and broke his thigh (Anon., 1906, January 11, *Freeman's Journal*, p. 15). In 1932, John Ryan TD, proposed it as an Olympic Venue for aquatic sports (Anon., 1932, August 31, *Irish Independent*, p. 8).

On ridicule of golf (Maume, P., 2007, 'Nationalist Attitudes to Golf', *History Ireland*, 15(1), 11).

The designation Royal was granted by Queen Victoria who had visited the area.

On course territory (Anon., 1908, May 29, *The Irish Times*, p. 3).

On prosecutions (Anon., 1903, February 5, 'Horse and van in the sea', *Freeman's Journal*, p. 12).

Legal entitlements to the island have fluctuated. Certainly in a dispute with the Port and Docks Board, the Vernons had successfully claimed possession of some of the island and its ever growing foreshore, with the P&DB restricted mostly to the wall. And John Vernon had kept cattle on the island until his death in 1890. John Vernon's successor, Colonel Vernon, after keeping cattle on the island for a year, rented, then sold the land to Lord Ardilaun who by 1902 seems to have wanted to build two golf courses and a bridge at the east end (Anon., 1902, June 9, *Freeman's Journal*). Further complicating legal ownership issues was the fact that at some point Colonel Vernon and Lord Howth split possession of parts of the island with a fence (Anon., 1900, May 17, *Freeman's Journal*, p. 3).

On dual membership (Anon., 1909, October 5, 'Bull Wall Bathing', *Freeman's Journal*, p. 4).

There were two battles at Le Cateau. Moran apparently died in a German Hospital following fighting in 1918 (Anon., 1954, August 30, 'Ireland's second oldest golf course', *Irish Independent*, p. 2). See also www.irishgolfarchive.com.

During the First World War the island was peaceful enough for the common tern to nest on it, something they were less likely to do when Kennedy was writing in 1953 (Kennedy, 1953).

Artificial dykes and drainage of the greens commenced as early as 1924 (O'Reilly, H.O. and Pantin, G., 1956/1957), 'Some observations on the salt marsh formation in Co. Dublin', *Proceedings of the Royal Irish Academy. Section B: Biological, Geological and Chemical Science*, 58, 89-128). Helen O'Reilly's obituary reads that she was active for many years promoting measures to preserve and safeguard habitats on the Bull (Jackson, P., 1988, 'Helen O'Reilly: 1922 to 1987', *The Irish Naturalists' Journal*, 22(11), 461-463).

On feeding starlings (Kennedy, 1953).

On golfers and birds (Anon., 1931, September 3, *Irish Independent*, p. 7).

St Anne's originally used a tin shack as a clubhouse.

The Royal's one-story clubhouse was renovated in 1901 and rebuilt in 1909 (Anon., 1954, August 30, 'Ireland's second oldest golf course', *Irish Independent*, p. 2). Gogarty states that port workers cottages stood on the original site (Gogarty, 2013).

On flames (Anon., 1943, August 2, 'Many escape in Dublin Golf Club Blaze', *Irish Independent*, p. 3).

The 1954 clubhouse was described as less pretentious by bird watcher Kennedy.

In the past the unions had been denied permission to erect tents.

On expropriated land (Anon., 1955, December 14, 'Golf club plan at Bull Island', *Irish Press*, p. 2).

On notice given (Anon., 1956, August 14, 'Bull Island Warning to Golf Club', *Irish Press*, p. 1).

On application for 18 holes (Anon., 1957, May 27, *Irish Press*, p. 3).

On car silencers (Anon., 1962, October 28, *Sunday Independent*, p. 7).

On species numbers (Healy, B., 1975, 'Fauna of the Salt-Marsh, North Bull Island, Dublin', *Proceedings of the Royal Irish Academy*, 75, 225-244). For copepods see also (O'Riordan, C.E., 1971, 'Meiobenthic Harpacticoida on the East Coast of Ireland'. *Proceedings of the Royal Irish Academy. Section B: Biological, Geological and Chemical Science*, 71, 191-210).

On 55 acres (Anon., 1965, October 14, *Irish Press*, p. 11).

On the people's property (Anon., 1964, April 14, *Irish Press*, p. 11).

On public rights (Anon., 1964, October 6, *Irish Press*, p. 4; Anon., 1964, October 16, *Irish Press*, p. 9).

On a gift from God (Anon., 1964, December 3, *Irish Press*, p. 11).

On deluge of letters (Anon., 1965, September 15, *Irish Press*, p. 5). Labour Councillor Rory Cowan, who had help set up the Bull Island Protection Association, later resigned in protest at his party's position (Anon., 1967, February 18, 'Eleventh Hour Strike', *Irish Press*, p. 9).

On fighting all the way (Anon., 1967, October 17, *Irish Press*, p. 9).

On a serious breach (Anon., 1973, July 13, *Irish Press*, p. 3).

On minister for local government (Anon., 1975, May 21, *Irish Press*, p. 7).

On general purposes committee (Anon., 1982, May 6, *Irish Press*, p. 9).

Asparagus was also observed in 1917 (Anon., 1917, 'Irish societies', *The Irish Naturalist*, 26(10), pp. 166-168).

On arson (Anon., 1982, April 9, *Irish Press*, p. 7).

On letter from Norton (Anon., 1982, April 27, *Irish Press*, p. 8).

Irrespective of the protesters attacks, St Anne's had always been subject to a certain level of petty crime; e.g. one Patrick Kenny broke in and stole eight golf balls in 1938 (Anon., 1938, September 8, 'Golf ball charge', *Irish Independent*, p. 10). Similarly in 1951, thieves stole £250 worth of cigarettes and whisky. Not that members were beyond their own petty crimes: the club was fined after the discovery of late night whiskey drinking and card playing by men and women in the same year (Anon., 1951, 'Golf club fined', *Irish Press*, p. 5). The Royal Dublin also suffered various incidents. In 1959, for example, thieves stole a telephone coin box, brandy and sherry (Anon., 1959, April 10, 'Drinks haul', *Irish Press*, p. 7).

On dispute ending bitterly (Anon., 1982, April 30, *Irish Press*, p. 7).

On artificial area (Anon., 1990, September 8, *Irish Press*, p. 13).

On resolution (Anon., 1982, June 22, *Irish Press*, p. 3). Trouble flared again briefly when the club removed 100 truckloads of sand from the beach to construct new fairways, leading environmentalists to fear for the viability of the dunes themselves (displaying Machiavellian levels of complicity, or simply ecological ignorance, the corporation said the sand was not leaving the island but being moved from one area to another).

On bird lore (Kennedy, 1953).

On Thomas McGun (Anon., 1955, October 14, 'Man dead in car on golf links', *Irish Press*, p. 9).

36

View from the Beach

Today on the beach, kite surfers, kite flyers and kite yachts take advantage of the island's strong breezes. Looking down the beach to the island's northern tip, the eye sweeps along the arch of sand to the isthmus at Sutton – over which you can make out the peak of an island called Ireland's Eye (on which William Kirwan supposedly murdered his wife Sarah with a sword cane in 1852). On route to the 567 feet high summit at Howth the eye next catches a Martello tower built around 1804 to keep Napoleon at bay (though he never showed up), the Green Bailey and finally the summit. From there, on a clear day you can see the entire bay, and even Wales.

In 1785, Richard Crosbie appears to have had an equally lofty view of the bay, when he rushed to the heavens in his new-fangled hot air balloon. Fearing he might cross the channel – an eventuality for which he was entirely unprepared – he opened the vents and ditched his scientific marvel on the Clontarf strand – apparently not drowning because it was low tide. Of late, nothing has descended in a manner that matches the dizzying science of that era, although some plants such as glasswort, devils bit and crow garlic are alien on the eye, and almost look like they could only be technology from another planet (where one might also imagine alien radio archaeologists listening to Kennedy's 1930 radio broadcasts on ornithology).

Passing from Howth, the gaze next launches out across six glorious miles of bay, following the horizon. In 1817, the bay was considered sufficiently beautiful to be comparable to the Bay of Naples, but owing to the decline in the reputation of Naples (waste collection horrors) this comparison is not mentioned much in Dublin anymore. The gaze arrives at Dalkey Island on the southern side, lingers on the breasts of the Dublin and Wicklow mountains, then pulls low and short to Dublin's famous and ever dominant candy striped 'Pigeon house' chimneys. In 1912, the smoke and haze of the city burning fossil fuels was such that the base of the Dublin and Wicklow Mountains was obscured, but with the dirty fuel ban much of the visible haze has dissipated. The gaze returns at last to the island's shore. Here we meet sleeping seaweed and whispering sand. And plastic – lots of plastic.

View From the Beach – Notes

In 1798, rebels would muster at night on Clontarf strand to plan their insurrection (Walsh, 1851).

On Crosbie (Urban, S., 1785, *The Gentleman's Magazine*, Vol. 57).

The Pigeon house chimneys: so called because one Mr Pigeon had an inn of sorts nearby – passing a levy on passengers docking at the 'packet station' there (later an artillery store) became known as plucking the pigeons.

37

Flotsam and Jetsam

Litter curses the island. It clings to the sorrowful marram grass; it soils the beach like wet toilet paper, which it sometimes is. It includes bottles, chemical containers, baby seats, items of clothing, food packaging, torn fishing nets and old Christmas trees. It comes from pedestrians, car owners and the sea itself: as far back as 1891, the Bailey lighthouse keeper had observed gulls following the 'Hopper' barges, such as the *Eblana*, as they dumped mud and street sweepings into the bay on an almost daily basis.

In the hot summer of 1948, a wildfire caused by a smoker seriously impacted the Bull's marram grass, prompting ISPB president T.H. Mason to lecture the public that cigarettes and matches should not be cast into the dry grass, bracken or heather (Howth experienced a serious fire around the same period). The fire could, of course, have been due to the abundant discarded glass. Either way, the lesson wasn't learned: gorse fires were extinguished again by firemen in 1967 and remain a threat today.

Sometime around June 1970, Dublin City Council, pressured for space and snubbing an active recycling policy, began to dump city refuse on the salt marsh. This went against its own development plans. It also flew in the face of bird protection acts – 29,700 birds had been counted on the island that winter. The city wanted to dump 27 acres of rubbish five feet high, weakly insisting it would cover it with topsoil and then make a park with shelters – for bird watchers. In fact, it wanted to facilitate further development on the island. Well aware of its destructive nature, the city planned and initiated the action in secret, reneging on earlier promises to consult with interest groups. In subsequent court hearings, it would refuse to reveal important documents to environmentalists.

Shocked conservationists argued that it would result in anoxic conditions in the wildfowl feeding areas, among other things. In January 1971, 30 members of Bull Island Protection Association blocked five lorry loads of refuse in one hour alone. Public outcry ensued, but the then Fianna Fáil Minister, Bobby Molloy, claimed he was powerless to intervene.

In February 1972, a temporary six-week court injunction was nevertheless secured by objectors at the Irish High Court. International support was also mustered in the same year at an international conference for the Conservation of Wetlands and Water Fowl held in Iran, which formally issued a recommendation for the conservation of the island. An Taisce led a comprehensive High Court challenge. The trust argued that the city had failed to follow its own planning requirements to preserve the amenity values of Dublin Bay. Judgement came in early 1973. An Taisce lost.

By February 1973, walkers on the causeway would write about the revolting smell emanating from all things rotting. Cans, cartons and bottles cascaded down the banks of the road. Eutrophication spawned toxic algae blooms. In 1975, the legal situation unexpectedly reversed. Fearing the increasingly likely success of a High Court appeal, the corporation finally agreed to stop dumping on the island. In a face-saving exercise, the corporation agreed not to carry out any development or 'reclamation' work until an environmental impact study by the state's Foras Forbartha was conducted.

Environmentalists scored a further success when the island was made a UNESCO biosphere in 1981. In addition to acknowledging the island's heaving biodiversity, this environmental designation (the first of many) was almost certainly a political attempt by international environmentalists to ward off further damage on the then world's smallest 'biosphere'. For a nation short on confidence and hungry for international recognition, this was not without some effect. And documentary footage from naturalist Gerrit van Gelderen (1926-1994) in his series *To the Waters and the Wild* now had a different context to footage ten years earlier.

For all that, in 1981, Michael Óg, a Young Scientist of the Year winner, could still observe old motor cars, rusty springs and broken glass. You can still see car parts today. This is not surprising. The dump was never entirely removed; much was covered over. It lies mostly under the sands at the interpretive centre and the causeway roundabout. At times it becomes visible. At the exhibition of Dublin Amateur and Artists Society of 1888 one Mr Inglis had exhibited a painting 'on the North Bull', whose good waves won special attention. In 1909, Wakeman's *On the North Bull* would picture bracken and 'other wild outcomes from the soil'. By 2010, in contrast, such aestheticism was impossible to consider without taking into account the human detritus. Even though a plastic bag tax had significantly reduced plastic bags on the beach, photographer

Dave Walsh's work firmly focused on discarded objects. The more notable were an armchair, a wooden chair, a ladder, a football, a wooden door and the remains of a TV.

Flotsam and Jetsam – Notes

In 1977, first year pupils of Holy Child school Killiney wrote a letter to the *Irish Press* expressing shock at amount of litter to be seen. The paper titled it 'Island of Litter' (Anon., 1977, June 2, 'Island of litter', *Irish Press*, p. 8).

Marram grass was sometimes planted to stop dune degradation (Irish Sea Study Group, 1990, *Irish Sea Study Group Report: Nature Conservation*, Liverpool University Press).

On the Eblana (Barrington, 1900).

On Mason's warning (Anon., 1948, April 3, 'Ornithologists', *Southern Star*, p. 4).

There appears to have been quite a bit of glass. In 1967, a story about two children cutting their feet on glass made the front pages (Anon., 1967, June 19, *Irish Press*, p. 1). In 'Lament for Bull Island', the poet Kevin Faller writes 'the dunes are sown with broken glass' (Faller, 1973).

On fires (Anon., 1967, April 17, 'Firemen busy at gorse fires', *Irish Press*, p. 1).

'Development plans' is meant in the wider sense. The city appears to have had no active management plan for the island itself at this time. The nature reserve was criticised as being merely a non-shooting area (Lang, J. T. and O'Rourke, F. J., 1970, 'Conservation of the Environment in Ireland', *An Irish Quarterly Review*, 59(235), 279-300).

An estimated 40,000 tonnes of material was dumped in the end (Anon., 1972, December 9, *Irish Press*, p. 3). The dump covered a 'substantial acreage'.

On secret actions (Anon., 1971, January 26, 'Bull Island Dumping', *The Irish Times*, p. 13).

On anoxic conditions (Fahy, E., 1976, 'Ireland's dumping dilemmas', *New Scientist*, January 8, p. 73).

Anon., 1971, January 23, 'Lorries on the way to Bull Island stopped', *The Irish Times*).

Anon., 1971, February 9, '6-week halt to island dumping', *The Irish Times*).

On international support (Anon., 1972, March 16, 'Clean Living', *Irish Press*; Anon., 1972, 'International conference on the conservation of wetlands and waterfowl', *International Legal Materials*, 11(5), pp. 963-976).

Anon., 1973, February 1, 'An Taisce Loses Action About Bull Island Dump', *The Irish Times*).

Anon., 1973, February 1973, 'Gassy smell', *Irish Times*, p. 6.

Foras Forbartha: The National Institute for Physical Planning and Construction Research.

On UNESCO award (Anon., 1981, December 25, *Irish Press*, p. 9).

On documentary footage (Anon., 1982, Apr 8, *Irish Press*, p. 19). Gerrit van Gelderen was a long time Bull supporter; in 1970, both he and Éamon De Buitléar had earlier collaborated on 'In defence of the Bull' in the series *Amuigh faoin Speir* (Out under the sky). The Bull Wall also briefly appears in Peter Lennon's 1952 film *Rocky Road to Dublin*.

On Inglis (Anon., 1888, January 24, 'Dublin Amateur and Artists Society', *The Irish Times*).

On Wakeman (Anon., 1909, October 5, *Freeman's Journal*, p. 4). In 1966, Johnathan Wade also painted 'Bull Island at night' (Anon., 1966, February 1, *Irish Press*, p. 9).

38

Bad Chemistry

It is hard to imagine air pollution on Bull Island. The winds are, at times, fresh and fierce. And yet, by 1977 the growth of the oakmoss on the trees in the Alder marsh was stunted due to air pollution. The moss was rare and scarce for the same reason. No better was the water pollution. Three streams debouche into the mudflats of the island: The Santry, the Kilbarrack and the Naniken (*Abhann-na-gCian*). The Santry, once flowing from the refuse dump at Edenmore, was likely the most toxic. Today the toxins are ever more complex, and the effects of their interactions ever more worrying. Yet in the waters here they are diluted to magnitudes difficult to detect with the naked eye – and the state shows no urgency in trying to test for them.

Visible pollution tends to fare slightly better. At least as far back as 1937, oil refineries were recognised as a threat to the birds of Bull Island. And even the Port and Docks Board regulated against the discharge of oil from ships or premises. However, regulation without enforcement is not a magic wand. In December 1942, a scaup duck was spotted at the edge of the salt marsh, badly oiled on the breast – from oil washed up in recent storms. Similarly, a year earlier a Razorbill was found badly oiled. In 1948, an oiled Kittiwake was also recorded, and so forth.

In 1976, Friends of the Earth campaigned against a proposed refinery at the port, citing it as a threat to Bull Island. Human error was always possible, and it would be impossible for Bull Island to escape the effects of a spillage. Sean Dublin Bay Loftus further revealed that Clontarf Yacht Club had been promised a new marina on the Bull Wall. This would be in exchange for not objecting to the reclamation plans of the Dublin Port and Docks Board for a massive oil and chemical storage zone adjacent to the island. The resultant furore from Clontarf to Sutton persisted well after the idea was officially denied. The claim, however, was probably not without foundation. As early as 1969, the Irish Wild Bird Conservancy (the trading name of Birdwatch Ireland), had warned of plans to reclaim the mudflats between the port and the Bull Wall.

On 30 January 2004, a diesel spill into one of the island's tributary rivers briefly threatened the island. A member of the public had spotted it on a Thursday evening, and raised the alarm. At first light, the area was cordoned off by a special boom. Fuel which had washed up on the island was vacuumed up with a special tanker, apparently with no harm done to the birds. The island was closed for the duration of the operation.

Sometimes harm to the island come from more benign sources. First discovered in 1934, the invasive rice grass spartina had been deliberately planted in straight lines in 43 separate locations (coincidentally or not, this followed the desire expressed by Rev. Kennedy in 1933 to see the island planted with low shrubs). The rapid growth of one variant quickly threatened the mudflats and was accelerated by the silting provoked by the causeway. From around 1970, *all* the spartina was regularly clipped (causing it to spread), dug up (where it spread during transportation) and sprayed with herbicides known as Dalapon and Hyvar X, whose adjacent environmental toxicity never seems to have been measured (the roots of the invasive buckthorn also continues to be injected with contentious herbicides such as Roundup). In 1981, the North Dublin Wildlife Group and the Irish Wildlife Federation would continue to manually battle the grass with 'a spartina pull'. But even with an enlightened method, nature does not rewind easily.

Bad Chemistry – Notes

The Alder marsh was first named informally by bird watchers in the 1930s who had spotted Alder saplings.

Evernia prunastri (Oakmoss) is a kind of lichen (Jeffrey, 1977). Lichen on the island is mostly grey; Mathilda C. Knowles reported *Candelariella epixantha* on maritime rocks at Dollymount in 1928, and *Lecanora Hageni* on the wooden railings in Dollymount in 1927 (Knowles, M., 1929, 'The lichen of Ireland', *Proceedings of the Royal Irish Academy. Section B: Biological, Geological, and Chemical Science*, 38(4), 179-434).

De Courcy names the river at Kilbarrack as Fox River (De-Courcy, 1996).

In 1912, the Naniken met the shore after passing under the Naniken Bridge (Weston St John Joyce, 1912).

In 1912, the river Santry discharged at the shore under Watermill Bridge, where a small mill once stood (Weston St John Joyce, 1912). A 1902 map labels the location watermill cottage. It is thought to have been part of a sixteenth century Dower House. There was also a 'light house at the piles on Raheny Wind Mill' noted by Scale and Richards in 1765 (Scale, Bernard and Richards, William, 1765). The mill, which is also present in the Down Survey of 1658, was described as being in ruins by Rocque in 1757. On the mainland here there was a marsh known as Watermill Lane Marsh, which was destroyed by the dumping of cement and boulders from local building work. Traces of it could still be found in 1956 (O'Reilly, H. O. and Pantin, G., 1956/1957, 'Some observations on the salt marsh formation in Co. Dublin', *Proceedings of the Royal Irish Academy. Section B: Biological, Geological and Chemical Science*, 58, 89-128).

On oil threat (Anon., 1937, May 12, 'Protectors of the birds', *Irish Independent*, p. 6).

On oiled Kittiwake (Kennedy, 1953).

On FOE campaign (Anon., 1976, January 20, *Irish Press*, p. 8).

On reclamation plans (Anon., 1976, April 16, *Irish Press*, p. 4; Anon., 1977, January 4, *Irish Press*, p. 6).

Two types of spartina were planted, *S. townsendii* and *S. Anglica*, which in turn created a variant known as *Spartina maritima forma dublinensis* (Jeffrey, 1977).

On Kennedy (Anon., 1933, August 23, 'Success of bird sanctuary', *Irish Independent*, p. 7).

The buckthorn spread rapidly after being planted along the boundaries of the golf course. The corporation has not removed it, and one ecologist in private conversation estimates that it could take over the island in as little as 50 years.

On spartina pull (Anon., 1981, May 29, 'North Bull Island', *Irish Press*, p. 11).

39

Art Deco

In 1874, an anonymous 'old salt' wrote to *The Irish Times*, requesting a committee be formed to erect wooden shelters to protect bathing clothes from rain. By 1905, people were still requesting a shelter (and paving), though nobody seemed keen to pay for it. The possibility of building a shelter along the wall around the 4,000 feet mark re-emerged as a more definite proposal in 1907. By June 1909, a Bathers' Association pushed to secure bathing shelters using 'open air parliaments'. It sought equal status with other UK ratepayers and equal treatment for women. The association argued that bathing, which was perceived as a natural right, had more than leisure benefits – it had health benefits. Many volunteered to be caretakers of the shelter. And in the end this agitation, awash with political undertones, secured the shelters.

But those shelters are not the ones that are there now. In 1934, the winds of the International Style blew over the island, and entered the mind of Herbert Simms, housing architect to Dublin City Corporation. When they had departed, a kiosk and a number of more solid bathing shelters graced the Bull Wall. Superficially, they bring to mind the

Art Deco movement but reflect the modernist ideology: ornament is a crime, truth to materials, form follows function. Their original naked and unornamented concrete has given way to paint, first white and now a thick and sea haggard sand colour. But unlike some of the later building on the island, the cut of these elegant structures pleases even the eye unversed in architecture. And though neglected and worn, they still exude an ineffable sentience.

One such shelter – a men's bathing shelter – is open and facing the sea, with its back to the island. A small entrance bolded MENS BATHING SHELTER leads down into a viewing and changing area. This, in turn, gives way to a carpet of descending steps, which change from concrete above the water mark to verdant green and bubbling seaweed. When the tide is out, you step on to a slim but gracious wisp of golden sand and broken shells.

When the tide is in, hardy swimmers ought to step off the steps into the invigorating bay waters. Yet for the most part this shelter lies empty. As do all the others. Aside from a few hardy souls, Dubliners now fear the waters of the bay will make them sick.

Art Deco – Notes

The 'old salt' complained that manure works had tainted water elsewhere on north side (Anon, 1874, May 20, 'The closing up of the North Bull', *The Irish Times)*. Possibly a source of inspiration for Joyce's old salt (see below)?

Bands played, and crowds of up to 5,000 could be present on the Bull Wall.

On open air parliaments (Anon., 1910, April 16, *The Irish Times*). The port board wanted indemnity from accidents among its many excuses. The port board claimed it did not have the authority to allow others to collect tolls for funding various items, and that the bridge was too shaky for events to be held on the wall. A plan for springboards never materialised. The bathers later agitated for a pleasure lake at Fairview.

The Bathers' Association was also known as the North Bull Bathers' Association; observations were made that some of the reluctant Port Board were also members of the Royal Dublin (Anon., 1909, October 5, 'Bull Wall Bathing', *Freeman's Journal*, p. 4).

Elsewhere in Dublin Simms also designed places like Henrietta House and St Audoen's House (http://dublinbay.wordpress.com/bull-wall-art-deco-bathing-shelters).

Separate shelters for women were built.

By 1947, freshwater taps at intervals along the seaward-facing dunes (some 30 feet high) were also installed (Farrington, A. and Haughton, J.P., 1947, April, 'The North Bull Island', *The Irish Naturalists Journal*, 9(2), 46-48).

40

Star of the Sea

Just past the bathing shelters, on the end of the Bull Wall, stands an imposing sculpture by Irish artist Cecil King, better known internationally for his minimalist paintings. Some seventy feet tall, this sculpture now goes by the of *Realt na Mara* or Star of the Sea. On the same promontory end, Second World War anti-aircraft guns were once positioned.

The sculpture was first proposed in 1950 at a Dockers retreat as a tribute to the Mother of God. It was intended to appear in the Marian year of 1954. But with rapid falloff in Docker's subscriptions, and tardy support from the frequently petitioned celestial being herself, it didn't get built until 1970. And if it hadn't been for the obsessional fundraising force of such Marian devotees as one William Nelson, it probably wouldn't have been built at all.

The finished sculpture is ostensibly a statue of the Virgin Mary, and so is also known as 'Our Ladies Memorial'. But in essence it mixes the kitsch of a lost Irish religiosity with *War of the Worlds*. Mary herself is not the problem; she looks more or less like every other star haloed Mary with a weathered face (well aside from the Waterford crystal stars). But the scale of her pedestal – a domineering tripod and orb on a base of Connemara marble – is inhuman. She has become an unintentional symbol of all that failed in the myopic Catholicism of the 1950s – a space incapable of breeding nostalgia. And rather incredibly, this is a scaled-down version of the original vision, a fact made all the more odd because Cecil King, as noted, was a minimalist. At one stage she was even floodlit in a kryptonite green.

Somewhat appropriately, the darkness below her fills with Dublin's sinners. When the eye adjusts, junkies, rent boys and Dublin's underworld laugh in the shadows. In 1969 – as part of a Gardaí sting – a Trinity professor waited nearby for a lucked out thief who had promised to deliver an ancient relic he had stolen from the college – the so-called harp of Brian Bóru.

But it is not always dark. In a clear night sky Cygnus – the Swan – is still half visible through the city's light pollution. And on the beach you can still make out the stranded moon jellyfish. In 1988, it would have been impossible to miss a giant, 70-foot long Gulliver lying on his back on the beach in commemoration of Jonathan Swift.

Star of the Sea – Notes

The association of Mary with the sea goes way back. *Ave Maris Stella* was a Latin plainsong popular in the Middle Ages.

On Second World War (Lynch, 2007). A mine also floated ashore in 1941 (Anon., 1941, February 6, 'Mine washed ashore', *Irish Independent*, p. 4). The military refused to comment.

Strictly speaking, *Realt na Mara* was not the first monument proposed. In 1885, an *Irish Times* cartoonist caricatured a nationalist suggesting that Nelson's Pillar be removed to Bull Island (Anon., 1885, October 24, 'Nelson or Brian', *The Irish Times*, p. 5).

Realt na Mara was built by builder William Lacey with the expertise of consulting engineer Bernard Le Cesne-Byrne. The selection of Cecil King was Lacey's idea.

Among the numerous other devotees were Ellen Dalton, William Rattigan and Louis Dixon. Nelson apparently saved several people from drowning during his lifetime.

Cecil was asked to seek inspiration from a somewhat uninspiring miraculous medal. The tripod was also mandated. The stainless steel halo, with 12 Waterford glass stars, was a later addition.

The recovered harp did not belong to Bóru, though it was a few centuries old. Over 50 Gardaí waited nearby. A second man was caught later (Anon., 1969, April 18, *Irish Press*, p. 1).

The giant Gulliver was not the strangest apparition. Hundreds of people jogging for charity dressed as Santa Claus probably win that one – although red does scare the birds.

Swift is known to have been in the locality in his lifetime (Gogarty, 2013).

Mahony, R., 1995, '250th Anniversary: Jonathan Swift as the "Patriot Dean"', *History Ireland*, 3(4), pp. 23-27.

41

Bottle Quay

Sutton Creek is the name given to the arching inlet of sea between the northern tip of the Island and Sutton Strand. It stretches around behind the island and past Kilbarrack Churchyard on the mainland (where nine bodies washed ashore from the ill-fated *Frederick* were buried in 1803). It continues past the area known as the black sands, until its natural flow is blocked at the causeway. Closer to the island's northern tip, an inlet on the shore opposite Sorento is known to locals as Bottle Quay. The oyster beds present here in 1756 are long gone.

When the tide goes out here, the Bull sands reappear, Sutton Creek diminishes, and it almost looks like you could walk from the island to either Sutton or the main Howth Road. This would be an error of judgement. In the year 1849, one Doctor Carmichael was drowned, when riding from the North Bull across the strand to his residence at Sutton (despite earlier warnings by a local, one E. Hogan). Ditto for 30-year-old unemployed carpenter John Hosier who, in 1886, went down in a deep channel trying to cross the strand on foot to Sutton.

The drowned carpenter's umbrella was mistaken for a child. The sources of this error were some women who first spotted the man in trouble. They also thought they saw a boy. Coincidentally, the women reported this fact to the same E. Hogan who had earlier warned Carmichael (and indeed also recovered Carmichael's body). Through opera glasses, Hogan watched the man, a strong swimmer, working against the strong ebb tide. Hogan sent his son to affect a rescue, but when the son's boat reached the area, all that was remained was a floating hat.

The sands are not without further evidence of nature's indifference to man. In 2001, at 6.00 am, a low spring tide allowed a fleeting glimpse of the skeleton of a boat with oaked planks and ribbed beams. A seventeenth century shipwreck. It had been disturbed during the dredging phase of a pipeline project – parts including the keel had come ashore on Bull Island. There are 300-400 wrecks detailed in the bay. This was not one of them. The uncharted wreck was 150 feet long, about the same length as the tall ship *Jeannie Johnston*, which now sits on the Liffey. Holes in the oak, made by sea lice, suggest that it may have participated in international trade. Little else is yet known about it. And in accordance with modern archaeological standards, it remains in the sand. Right now, the past is not recoverable.

Bottle Quay – Notes

On the *Frederick* (Brady, K., 2008, p. 221).

The mainland banks arching on the easterly road towards Sutton – where the Howth Road meets the coast – were once known as the black sands or blank banks.

Sand barring access to Sutton Creek was once known as the Sutton Bar (De Courcy, 1996).

On Carmichael (Anon., 1877, June 27, *The Irish Times*).

On Hosier (Anon., 1866, September 24, 'The case of drowning at the North Bull', *The Irish Times*).

Similarly, the body of a drowned man, possibly one Edward Stratten, also washed up at the black banks in 1865 (Anon., 1865, August 11,.' The recent boat accident', *The Irish Times*).

A small portion of the unidentified wreck went to wet storage. This contrasts with the fate of an ancient canoe found in the Sutton sands in the early twentieth century. It was pulled from the sands like an old tooth.

42

The Seals

The water around Bull Island has long been home to mammals such as the common porpoise and the white-beaked dolphin. But mostly it is known for its seals, which often come from caves at nearby Howth. In 1829, scientist Robert Ball took a boat to the caves, to observe them pass like globules of mercury beneath it. He later reported to the Royal Irish Academy that he had succeeded in killing a very large grey seal that 'was a female and appeared to be suckling her young at the time'. In 1839, fisherman Henry Sword found a seal at the North Bull devouring a fish in shallow water. He quickly got behind it and beating it to the shore with a rope 'succeeded in making it his prize'. The 'fine specimen', more interesting dead than alive, was promptly put on display at the Portobello Zoological Gardens.

In 1873, *The Irish Times* reported large quantities of seals remained near the nose of Howth and Bailey Lighthouse. The writer observed that country people formerly killed them in caves by night, although they had been left for some years un-molested; and that this might have increased their numbers. As the seals were so approachable – they were easily struck with a boat hook – the writer thought this may have been of interest to lovers of the rifle: better to have shot a fine seal than a dummy on the sand of the North Bull. Such behaviour was not idiosyncratic. By 1914, the number of grey seals in the entire waters of Great Britain was thought to have collapsed to a mere 500. Such low numbers alarmed sportsmen and lead to the introduction of the *Grey Seal Protection Act* in the same year.

In 1924, however, with independence secured for Ireland, a meeting of the Dublin Board of Conservators – aiming to conserve fish stock – confirmed that rewards would be maintained for any seal killed within the North Bull lights. Charles Green, Minister of Fisheries in Dublin, wrote to George Hogarth of the Fisheries Board for Scotland that 'while you have been cherishing the brutes, we have been offering rewards for their destruction'.

Since then the seals have continued to suffer culls – the effects of overfishing – and pollution. But like a lot of things on the island, they received better legal protection when Ireland signed up in 1982 to the Convention on the Conservation of European Wildlife and Natural Habitats (the Berne Convention). The numbers for Ireland alone now stand at over 5,000. Not everything can be legally protected. As a result of climate change and overfishing in Greenland, the arctic harp seal has migrated further south. It carries the devastating Phocine Distemper Virus, and on occasion this further threatens the seals.

Local activists have fought long and hard to protect the seals. As with the birders, botanists and entomologists, their work is tireless and unending.

The Seals – Notes

On mammals (Jeffrey, 1977).

Ball, a member of the Royal Irish Academy, also reports that seals frequently swam up the Liffey, supposedly after herring (Ball, R., 1839, 'Remarks on the species of seals (Phocidae) inhabiting the Irish seas', *The Transactions of the Royal Academy*, 18, pp. 89-98).

On the fine specimen (Anon., 1839, October 29, *Freeman's Journal*, p. 4).

On shooting seals (Anon., 1873, December 20, *The Irish Times*).

On Dublin Conservators (Anon., 1924, October 23, 'Conservators of Fishing', *Freeman's Journal*, p. 8).

On Green (Lambert, R. A., 2002, 'The grey seal in Britain: A twentieth century history of a nature conservation success', *Environment and History*, 8(4), 449-74).

43

Biosphere

Bull Island is part of a global ecosystem. It cannot offer sanctuary by itself. It suffers from air pollution, water pollution and dumping from the city. Its animals have been shot, ferreted and hunted in every way possible. A virus from further afield devastated its rabbit population. Its migrant birds are tussled by local actions and events on the other side of the globe. Invasive plants have been introduced and the largely unmanaged buckthorn could soon over run the island. Climate change already affects its flora, fauna and mammals. With rising sea levels on their way, the sea might yet swallow whole this low lying island within our lifetime.

Bligh's association with the island seemingly symbolises the role engineers played in the island's formation. But the story of a heroic engineer building a wall that made an island belies the island's prehistory. It also masks a story of uncontrolled human activity on a vast scale, activity that could seemingly accelerate the growth of ever more treacherous sand banks and even destroy islands.

Nature's power remains chilling: in 1844, after a house on Clontarf Island disappeared in a storm, a different storm swept 'a great proportion' of the nascent Bull Island away. The island's many shipwrecks are a further awesome reminder of how terrifying nature can be to a culture whose technology is incapable of controlling it. In 1788, the crew of the *Favourite Nanny* could be seen desperately cutting away at the ship's masts as the sea rolled over it. At the same time, a collier that had hit the sands could be seen through a telescope drifting towards Howth with her crew lashed to the masts. In such a storm, nothing could be done to rescue them.

It is impossible to forget such people. But we should also remember the heroic and innumerable activists who fought to make this island a sanctuary for birds and wildlife. All those who cleaned up oil spills and litter, who fought to prevent the destruction of the habitat, who charted what we've lost and what we might lose, and whose campaigns dragged unceasingly through decades and generations, as they will continue to. The best way to remember them is to help continue this work. We are all ephemeral guardians; a thriving ecosystem is the only worthy memorial. This history is one of a special conservation area, but really it is the story of what is happening across Ireland and our planet.

The city's capacity to manage Bull Island is highly questionable, and it is self-evident to many that the island should actually be in the hands of the National Parks and Wildlife Service. But we must think through our actions carefully. Even in 1977, An Taisce's proposal to 'save' the island involved building a road down the middle of it. Similarly, in 2008 the bridge restoration project addressed the problem of rotting wood. In addition to the native Irish Douglas Fir, it uses Greenhart from Guyana and Ekki from West Africa. Greenhart is highly resistant to fungi, marine borers and dry-wood termites – and so a marine and shipbuilder's favourite. But the habitats of Ekki are now endangered, and in 1996 Greenheart was listed on the Red List of the International Union for the Conservation of Nature as vulnerable. We are not omniscient. 'First do no harm' remains the best guiding principal at our disposal.

On August 29, with no all clear but my ankle much improved, I cycle to the northern end of the island. Not far from some cormorants, I spy a solitary seal and her pup. We watch each other from a distance. My heart races with a cautionary and shameless pleasure. I stare at the seal for so long that for a brief moment I almost expect to become one with it. But this does not happen. When time returns, I turn and wheel the bike off through the detritus cast over the sands by humans. I am not at one with nature, but perhaps I am a little closer.

My breathing is getting short – it could always be the clot going to my lungs – but perhaps I have simply become unfit. I turn and look at my tracks and wheel marks stretching back into the past – untidy work for a historian – and think of all the problems that my children will have to understand and face with courage. I think of how I will teach Sadhbh not to add one of the island's precious and slow-growing orchids into her beautiful flower book. I think of how I might best help her and Hugh learn the language of this island. Of how I might help them see and understand in its short history the greater part of life's ceaseless wonder, challenges and fragility. And as time moves around and through me, I realise that some day they will understand I am with them always, and that the story of this island is part of my gift to them.

Biosphere – Notes

Erosion of the island was also speculated to have occurred by the island sinking or subsiding (O'Reilly, H.O. and Pantin, G., 1956/1957, 'Some observations on the salt marsh formation in Co. Dublin', *Proceedings of the Royal Irish Academy. Section B: Biological, Geological and Chemical Science*, 58, 89-128).

On sweeping away of island (Anon., 1844, November 9, 'The Gale of Friday and Saturday', *The Nation*, p. 4).

The *Favourite Nanny*, under captain Gunderton, had been bound for Bordeaux. A passenger Foster is mentioned. Another ship also struck the Bull in this storm (Anon., 1787, September 20, *Freeman's Journal*, p. 4). In 1799 the crew of one ship similarly lashed themselves to the rigging, but were found dead at Clontarf (Brady, K., 2008).

August 29 is my wife's birthday.

On the road (Jeffrey, 1977).

In 1906, Greenhart piles were being waited upon by bridge engineers (Anon., 1906, April 20. *Irish Independent*, p. 6).

Mid-twentieth century, Hassell listed around 100 kinds of fungi (Hassell, F. C., 1953, 'The Fungi of North Bull Island, Co. Dublin', *The Irish Naturalists' Journal*. 11(1), pp.3-7).

44

An Old Salt

An all knowing heron is watching. The tide returns, we are back to Joyce, back to Bloom:

On more than one occasion, a dozen at the lowest, near the North Bull at Dollymount he had remarked a superannuated old salt, evidently derelict, seated habitually near the not particularly redolent sea on the wall, staring quite obliviously at it and it at him, dreaming of fresh woods and pastures new as someone somewhere sings. And it left him wondering why. Possibly he had tried to find out the secret for himself, floundering up and down the antipodes and all that sort of thing and over and under, well, not exactly under, tempting the fates. And the odds were twenty to nil there was really no secret about it at all.